Refresh your

CLAUDIA
BARBA

A WOMEN'S BIBLE STUDY

journeyforth®

Greenville, South Carolina

Cover Photo Credits: Sebastian Duda/iStockPhoto.com

The fact that materials produced by other publishers may be referred to in this volume does not constitute an endorsement of the content or theological position of materials produced by such publishers.

All Scripture is quoted from the Authorized King James Version.

Refresh Your Heart
Claudia Barba

Design by Craig Oesterling
Page layout by Kelley Moore

© 2008 BJU Press
Greenville, South Carolina 29609
JourneyForth Books is a division of BJU Press.

ISBN 978-1-59166-849-7
eISBN 978-1-62856-391-7

15   14   13   12   11   10   9   8   7

Contents

Lesson 1 A Woman's Heart

Let's take a close look at your heart. The Bible uses the word *heart* to mean much more than the physical organ that pumps blood. It's the totality of you—your emotional, mental, and spiritual self. It needs to be guarded (by much more than your rib cage) because it is extremely important. It can also be dangerous, for it is the source of sin. But there's hope for every heart—including yours!

Know Your Heart

Your heart is your emotional self

1. Our language is full of phrases that describe the heart as the seat of emotions. For example, we talk about having a "broken heart." Can you think of other examples?

   _____

   _____

   _____

   _____

2. The Bible also describes emotions as dwelling in the heart. What emotions are attributed to the heart in these verses?

2 Samuel 6:16 _____

Psalm 4:7 _____

Psalm 13:2 _____

Psalm 27:3 _____

Psalm 73:21 _____

Psalm 143:4 _____

James 3:14 _____

Your heart is your thinking self

We speak of thought as taking place in the heart. We might say, "In my heart, I know he's right."

3. The Bible also talks about some mental processes as taking place in the heart. According to the following verses, what are they?

Proverbs 23:7

_____

Matthew 13:15

_____

Luke 2:19

_____

Acts 5:3–4

_____

2 Corinthians 9:7

_____

We know that words come through the brain and out of the mouth. But we also talk about words as coming from the heart—heartfelt words. According to Matthew 12:34–35, all words, sincere or deceitful, come from a good or an evil heart.

Out of the abundance of the heart the mouth speaketh. A good man out of the good treasure of the heart bringeth forth good things: and an evil man out of the evil treasure bringeth forth evil things.

4. Read Ephesians 5:19. What other kind of communication comes from the heart?

_____

_____

_____

5. What does Exodus 35:35 say about the source of all creativity?

_____

_____

Your words reveal whether your heart is good or evil. The music you love, the art you produce, and all other expressions of creativity reveal the condition of your heart.

Your heart is your spiritual self

6. You _____ God with your heart (Deuteronomy 4:29).

   You _____ God with your heart (Deuteronomy 6:5).

   You _____ God with your heart (Deuteronomy 11:13).

You also believe in God with your heart (Romans 10:9–10). Your conscience—moral sense of right and wrong—is seated in your heart.

7. The Old Testament (written in Hebrew) had no word for conscience, but the concept is there. How is it described in Job 27:6?

_____

_____

3

8. The New Testament also speaks of two different kinds of consciences as being linked with the heart. Circle the words that describe them.

   Having our hearts sprinkled from an evil conscience. (Hebrews 10:22)

   Now the end of the commandment is charity out of a pure heart, and of a good conscience. (1 Timothy 1:5)

9. What is really happening when we have those feelings and thoughts that we call "conscience" (1 John 3:20–21)?

   _____

   _____

GUARD YOUR HEART

10. Write out the important command of Proverbs 4:23.

    _____

    _____

11. To "keep" the heart is to guard it. How are you supposed to guard your heart, according to this verse?

    _____

12. Using a dictionary, define the word *diligence*.

    _____

    _____

13. The words in this verse depict a warden at his post "keeping" his prisoner. What does this teach you about your heart?

    _____

    _____

14. Why must you guard it diligently?

    _____

Guard it because it's important, for "out of it are the issues of life" (Proverbs 4:23)! All the important "issues of life" come straight from your heart because it is the source of your emotions, your thoughts, and your spiritual responses.

Also guard it because it's dangerous!

15. What awful news about the heart do we read in Jeremiah 17:9?

_____

_____

_____

You were born with a heart that is deceitful (fraudulent, crooked, polluted) and desperately wicked (incurably, dreadfully sick with sin). It is too defiled for explanation and so wicked that no one can understand it.

16. What specific sins come directly out of a heart like this, according to Mark 7:21–23? (Look up any unfamiliar words.)

_____

_____

_____

All this evil comes from _____ (verse 23).

So when you sin, whose fault is it?

_____

Read another sobering list—the "works of the flesh"—in Galatians 5:19–21. Many of these are physical sins, with roots in the emotional, mental, and spiritual depravity of the heart. Do any of these sins appear in your own life?

The sad truth is that "in me (that is, in my flesh,) dwelleth no good thing" (Romans 7:18).

HOPE FOR YOUR HEART

There's no need for despair. There is hope for your heart! Hope is not in reformation or in determining to be better. It's not in resolutions or willpower. In fact, every effort to change yourself by your own power will ultimately fail. Only God can permanently change you. He wants to, He can, and He will!

God works in your heart

God shows you your heart's need. Because the heart is the source of the problem of sin, it's the heart that is the focus of the Savior's attention. As His first step in changing you, He will show you the sin in your heart.

All people, whether they believe it or not, are subject to the law of God. Breaking God's law is sin. God's law is written down in His Word, the Bible. It is also revealed by nature.

17. According to Romans 2:14–16, where else is God's law written?

_____

What specific place in your heart tells you that you have sinned?

_____

The moment you most clearly see your own hopeless sinfulness, there is the most hope for you! When you realize that you need a Savior, He is there, ready to save you. Then comes hope, as God plants His Word in your heart.

Read Matthew 13:3–9 and 13:18–23.

18. What are the four different responses of hearts to the seed of the gospel? What happens to the seed planted there?

Wayside hearers

_____

Stony-ground hearers

_____

A Woman's Heart

Thorny-ground hearers

Good-ground hearers

When God sees that the seed of the gospel has fallen on good ground, He saves your believing heart.

19. Read Romans 10:9–10. Where do we believe "unto righteousness?"

---

20. What does this mean? As you answer, keep in mind the definition of the word *heart*.

You may have gone to church many years and know a lot about the Bible. You may have been baptized, confirmed, or physically healed or have had a stirring emotional experience. Do any of these experiences equal salvation?

Salvation comes when you understand that your heart is "deceitful above all things and desperately wicked," when you believe that Christ's death on the cross was the sufficient payment for all your sins, and at one special moment, you turn in repentance and faith to Jesus Christ and ask Him to save you.

Salvation is a heart change. This is the "new birth." It's being saved! No one is born saved or grows into salvation; it is a personal, one-time, once-for-all transaction with God.

21. When confession of sin and belief in Christ take place in your heart, what happens to you (2 Corinthians 5:17)?

7

Nothing is ever the same after that. It's not a moment you can be unaware of or forget. You will *know* when salvation has come to your heart.

Has this happened to you? Have you been saved? When did the Lord save your believing heart? Briefly write your testimony describing your time of salvation in the space provided on pages 127–30.

If you do not have a confident testimony or a clear memory of this important transaction with God, maybe you have not yet been made a "new creature." If not, you can be saved right now! Pray a prayer like this:

> Dear God, I know that I have a sinful heart and deserve eternal separation from You in hell. But right now I turn away from my sinful self and turn to You instead. I ask You to cleanse my sinful heart and make me a new creation. I trust Jesus Christ alone as my Savior from sin. Thank You for saving me. I give You my life and ask You to help me live for You.

If you have been saved, your old heart has been changed into a new heart that loves God and seeks to please Him. Only God can make a change like that. Praise Him!

God cleanses your heart

Wouldn't it be wonderful if salvation meant the end of sinning? It doesn't, though. In fact, after you have been saved, you will be more aware than ever of your sinfulness and need for continual cleansing. This is part of the ministry of the Holy Spirit—to convict you of sin. But the wonderful truth is that God will cleanse your repentant heart!

22. What absolute promise is given to believers in 1 John 1:9?

_____

_____

King David believed in Jehovah God, but he sinned and needed forgiveness. After his sin with Bathsheba, he experienced heavy guilt.

(Read 2 Samuel 11 if you are not familiar with this story.) Repenting, he prayed the prayer of a contrite heart, recorded for us in Psalm 51.

23. What attributes (character qualities) of God did David plead in verse 1?

_____

_____

24. What term in verse 1 did he use to describe his sin?

_____

Every sin is the breaking, or transgression, of God's law. First John 3:4 says, "Whosoever committeth sin transgresseth also the law: for sin is the transgression of the law."

Although David had sinned against Bathsheba and Uriah, his sin was ultimately against God. He had broken God's laws. He had coveted, lied, committed adultery, and murdered. But he still was not hopeless!

25. What did David ask God to do to his heart (verses 2, 7, 10)?

_____

_____

What emotions did he expect to experience after forgiveness (verses 8, 12)?

_____

_____

What was he planning to do when he was clean once more (verses 13-15)?

_____

_____

David was obviously not a perfect man, but he was called a man who had a heart like God's (1 Samuel 13:14; Acts 13:22). Maybe that was because of David's attitude toward his sin. He saw it as God sees it. He admitted it; in sorrow and contrition he sought forgiveness. That's the spirit of "a broken and a contrite heart" that God "wilt not despise" (Psalm 51:17).

Remember that your heart is *you*. Your emotional self. Your mental self. Your spiritual self. It must be guarded. It's important, as the source of all the issues of life.

It's dangerous because it is "deceitful above all things, and desperately wicked."

God works in your heart. He shows you your heart's need. He plants His Word in your heart. He saves your believing heart. He cleanses your heart. After salvation, He daily forgives and cleanses the sin in your heart.

Lesson 2 A Trusting Heart

A baby wakes from his nap. As his mother lifts him from his crib, he smiles and snuggles on her shoulder, relaxed and confident. He would not have the same reaction if a stranger appeared in his room. He feels secure with his mommy because he knows her. Because he knows her, he trusts her.

Just as a mother's arms are a safe place for a child, the heavenly Father's arms are a believer's refuge. Your trust in Him is based on your knowledge of Him. The more you know God, the more you will trust Him.

Does your heart trust God, believing that He is working out everything for your good? Or do you worry that He may make mistakes? If you're fretful, maybe the problem is that you do not fully know Him.

First, you must know Him as Savior and Lord. Following your salvation, learning all you can about His attributes will help you become His relaxed, confident child.

YOUR HEAVENLY FATHER IS *OMNISCIENT*

God knows everything. He sees all eternity at once: past, present, and future. He says, "I am God, and there is none else; I am God, and there is none like me, declaring the end from the beginning, and from ancient times the things that are not yet done" (Isaiah 46:9–10).

God, the all-knowing One, knows your history. He is aware of your present and has full understanding of your future.

God knows your past

You may be tormented by your personal history, even the moments over which you had no control. Looking back, you may conclude that during difficult days God was absent and did not know what was happening to you. But God does know all about your yesterdays, for He was there.

Maybe it's the circumstances of your birth and family background that trouble you and hinder your trust in God. If so, meditate on the following Bible truths: God gives children to specific parents. Discover that truth in the following verses.

> *Is anything too hard for the Lord? At the time appointed I will return unto thee, according to the time of life, and Sarah shall have a son. (Genesis 18:14)*

> *And [Esau] lifted up his eyes, and saw the women and the children; and said, Who are those with thee? And [Jacob] said, The children which God hath graciously given thy servant. (Genesis 33:5)*

> *Lo, children are an heritage of the Lord, and the fruit of the womb is his reward. (Psalm 127:3)*

God plans every child, including you. Psalm 139 makes this clear.

> *For thou hast possessed [created] my reins [internal organs]: thou hast covered me [joined me together] in my mother's womb. (verse 13)*

> *My substance [body] was not hid from thee, when I was made in secret, and curiously wrought [embroidered] in the lowest parts of the earth [a secret place—the womb]. (verse 15)*

> *Thine eyes did see my substance [embryo] yet being unperfect; and in thy book all my members were written [described] which in continuance were fashioned [molded, formed] when as yet there was none of them. (verse 16)*

1. Is any child born "by accident"? According to Psalm 139, what was the process of your birth (beginning before conception)?

_____

_____

When God finished making you, what did He think of you? Read Psalm 139:14 and write in your own words what both you and the psalmist David can truthfully say.

_____

_____

Perhaps it's the memory of past sins that haunts you. If so, remember this: If you have confessed those sins to your Father and asked for His forgiveness, they are gone! He has freely forgiven you of the guilt and penalty due for those sins. Read 1 John 1:7–9.

2. According to verse 7, what cleanses you from sin? Does forgiveness have anything to do with your own works or acts of penance?

_____

_____

3. How many of your sins are cleansed by His blood? Are there any left to atone for by yourself?

_____

4. According to verse 9, what is the only condition for your forgiveness (the only "if")?

_____

5. Two attributes of God are mentioned that guarantee His forgiveness. God is _____ and He is _____.

6. Who has removed your forgiven sins (Psalm 103:12)? Where are they? Where is that?

_____

_____

_____

When I was a little girl, my preacher father led a woman to Christ in our home and then asked to borrow my globe. I watched as he moved his finger along the equator to illustrate to her that the east never meets the west. I will never forget the joy on her face when she comprehended that her sins were gone forever. They had been removed to where east and west meet—which is nowhere!

7. According to Micah 7:18, our wonderful God is eager to pardon our sins, for He "delighteth in mercy." The next verse gives us another assurance of His forgiveness. Where has He cast our sins, according to this verse? Can a human being go there?

_____

Your forgiven sins are gone! They are completely covered by the blood of Jesus Christ, and God chooses to no longer remember them. You don't have to remember them, either!

God knows your present

8. Read Psalm 139:2–4. List the mundane activities of daily life that God knows.

_____

_____

_____

Read verses 8–12 of the same psalm. What places of escape did the psalmist mention? Could he succeed?

_____

_____

9. Do you know what attribute (characteristic or quality) of God this verse teaches? God is *omni*_____.

10. God knows where you are every moment; He is watching you. His purpose for doing this is not fearsome, but comforting instead. What is His purpose for keeping you in His sight (verse 10)?

_____

_____

11. When you are going through a tough time, a friend can help with the simple message "I'm thinking about you." Read verses 17–18. How often does your heavenly Father think about you?

_____

_____

When my son Jeremiah was little and learning to count, we read Psalm 139:17–18 together. He asked, "How many is that?" "How many is what?" I responded. "How many is the number of the sand?" "It's a lot," I assured him. "Can we count them?" he persisted. "Yes, we could count some," I agreed, thinking that he could use some counting practice. We got a cup of sand, a toothpick, a sheet of white paper, and a magnifying glass and began to count grains of sand. I quickly realized that this would take more time than we had and larger numbers than he knew. We decided to count just a spoonful. Still there were far too many. We finally decided to count just the grains of sand that stuck to one little finger and were then brushed onto the paper. That was manageable. "Forty-two!" he exclaimed when he was finished. "Did God think about me forty-two times today?"

The God of the universe doesn't think about you just forty-two times a day. His thoughts of you are continuous—He never stops! What's His purpose in thinking this much about you? See Proverbs 24:12.

God knows your future

You can trust your heavenly Father to meet every coming need. Women are experts at worrying about the future—at imagining all the horrid things that could happen! How comforting it is to know that the Lord can see all the way down the road and that He has anticipated every need. Just as long-distance hikers have supplies cached along their upcoming trail, you have supplies from His inexhaustible resources waiting along your path. They will be there for you, exactly when and where you need them.

12. What has God promised in Philippians 4:19?

_____

_____

13. How do you know He will never break this promise (Numbers 23:19)?

_____

_____

Two important commands are given in Matthew 6:33–34. Obeying them consistently will change your life.

14. The first one is in verse 33. Copy it here.

_____

_____

What does this command mean?

_____

_____

_____

What promise does He give to those who obey it?

_____

_____

What comes first in your morning schedule—the Scriptures and prayer, or breakfast, makeup, hair, watching the news, and checking the weather? Where do you primarily invest your time—in ministry through your church and to needy individuals, or to improving your house, shopping for clothes, and being entertained by videos and television? When you receive an unexpected sum of money, what is your first thought—spending it on luxuries or investing it in eternal causes?

15. The second command is in verse 34. What is it?

_____

_____

Your heavenly Father, Who knows what is ahead, has great promises for your future.

16. What do the following verses pledge for the days ahead?

    Proverbs 3:5–6_____

    James 1:5_____

    Isaiah 46:4_____

    Deuteronomy 33:25_____

When our daughter Susannah had chickenpox, the spots and itches were no fun for a busy six-year-old on the sunny summer days. Her friends came over daily to see if she were well enough to play. She soon felt fine but had a few more days to go before she would no longer be contagious. One afternoon I heard her telling her friends through the screen door: "I can't come out today, but on Thursday I won't be courageous!"

Thursday came very slowly for Susannah, but days seem to rush by me. And if the Lord should ever tell me what He has planned for some fast-arriving Thursday, I might say with Susannah, "But on Thursday I won't be courageous! I won't be able to face it; it will be too much for me!"

The Lord doesn't publish His agenda in advance, and I am glad. I would panic. But when the Thursdays of my life arrive, with their trials and challenges, I find that courage and grace have arrived along with them. There's strength to match every stress and peace in equal measure to pain. Today, I don't need next Thursday's courage. I need only enough for today. And all I need, He supplies.

YOUR HEAVENLY FATHER IS *OMNIPOTENT*

A friend, sister, or husband may sympathize but be helpless to solve your problems. God, however, can change your circumstances. As the ultimate Ruler of the universe, He can do anything. He has power!

He has power over nature

17. What natural elements are under His control? Read the following verses to see some of these elements.

    Isaiah 40:12_____

Jeremiah 10:13_____

Psalm 147:8–9, 16–18_____

Mark 4:41; Psalm 89:9_____

Revelation 4:11_____

Are thunderstorms, drought, floods, hurricanes, tornados, and other natural "disasters" out of His control? Nature should stimulate you to worship the Creator, not His creation.

18. Psalm 36:5–6 tells us that seeing the

heavens should remind you of His_____

clouds should remind you of His_____

mountains should remind you of His_____

the deep sea should remind you of His_____

We should think of nature not as something to be feared but as a reflection and reminder of our wonderful Father. No matter what natural events transpire, we can trust in the promise of Psalm 36:6— God keeps all men and animals safe!

19. What attribute of God motivates Him to do this (Psalm 36:7a)?

_____

20. Therefore, how should you react to events in nature that may concern or frighten you (Psalm 36:7b)?

_____

_____

He has power over people

21. Your Father has power over the people who have power over you! What do Proverbs 21:1 and Romans 13:1 say about the relationship between a political leader ("king") and God's divine hand?

_____

_____

Jesus Christ made His authority over human governmental authority unmistakable in a remarkable exchange with Pilate in John 19:9–11. Pilate threatened Jesus, asserting he had power to put Jesus to death. Jesus answered, "You could have no power at all unless it came from heaven." Even if rulers do not believe in our heavenly Father, He still exercises power over them and uses them to protect or chastise us. Political leaders are subject to God's rule.

He has power over angels

Good angels. Angels are God's servants. One of their assignments is *you!*

22. What specific tasks has God given His angels (Psalm 34:7)?

_____

_____

What, at this moment, are God's angels doing for you (Psalm 91:11)?

_____

Your kind, loving Father has provided you with these helpers and protectors. You can trust Him.

Evil angels. Demons are fallen angels—the angels who rebelled with Satan against God's authority (Revelation 12:9). Today they are opposing God's purposes and serving Satan in his efforts to hinder God's work in the world. They distress humans and propagate false doctrines. You ought to avoid any contact with satanism in any form. Satan and his angels are real; they seek your harm. But you do not have to have a paralyzing, unhealthy fear of them, for your Father has them under His command.

23. According to James 2:19 what do the devils (demons) know about God? How do they respond to Him?

_____

_____

In Matthew 8:28–29 and Mark 1:23–24, demons encountered Christ on the earth. They called Him "Son of God" and "the Holy One of

God." They feared He would send them to what they know is their ultimate destination: "everlasting fire, prepared for the devil and his angels" (Matthew 25:41). Demons are the already-defeated foes of God and His children. They are active in this world but face doom in the next. These ugly "powers of darkness" cannot harm you, the child of the God they fear. You can trust your Father to protect you from their attacks.

He has power over death

Unless the Lord returns in your lifetime, you will die. That is a fact you have to acknowledge and accept. But you don't need to fear death. For God's child, physical death is not the end of life; it is simply a passage from your earthly life to your heavenly life. Before dying, you are alive on the earth. After dying, you will be much more alive in heaven!

Death is simply moving "through the valley of the shadow of death" from one home to another. The instant you are "absent from the body" [physical death], you will be "present with the Lord" (2 Corinthians 5:8).

24. Read 1 Corinthians 15:12–22 and answer the following questions.

Why is Christ's resurrection so important?

_____

_____

What will be our emotional and mental state if we do not believe in the resurrection?

_____

_____

But Christ did rise again, and so will we, so there is no need for misery! Read verses 55–56. Death holds no more "sting" (poison prick) for a believer.

What a powerful God we have! He has power over nature, people, angels, even over death. You can trust Him.

YOUR HEAVENLY FATHER IS *LOVING*

You can trust God because He loves you. Do you believe that? Let's see if you qualify as one of the people He loves. Are you one of the people on the earth? If so, God loves you! Quote John 3:16, replacing "the world" with your own name. If this were the only verse in the Bible, it would be enough to prove God's love for you. But it isn't.

Are you a sinner? If so, God loves you! How do you know? Romans 5:8 says, "But God commendeth [showed] his love toward us, in that, while we were yet [still] sinners Christ died for us."

Are you a part of the body of believers, the church? If you are saved, you are! You are one of His special, "called out" ones, and He loves you! The Lord uses marriage as a metaphor of His loving relationship with us. Read Ephesians 5:25–29 to learn how sweetly He loves His church: "For no man ever yet hated his own flesh, but nourisheth and cherisheth it, even as the Lord the church."

25. Because He loves you, what are His goals for you, according to Ephesians 5:26–27?

   _____

   _____

   _____

   How should this change your attitude toward difficult life circumstances?

   _____

   _____

First John 4:8 tells us that "God is love." He is not merely loving; He *is* love. Love is His essence and His nature. As long as He is God, He will love, and He will love you. You can trust your loving Father!

Lesson 3 A Peaceful Heart

Has reviewing the attributes of God increased your confidence in Him? It's likely that none of the attributes we studied in the previous lesson were new to you. Most of us remember from our days in Sunday school that God is omniscient, that He is omnipotent, and that He is love.

Esther also knew all these truths about God. Her missionary parents explained them to her when she was a child. She in turn taught them to her own children. But during a family crisis, she found herself emotionally devastated. She lay on the couch for days, unable to dress, clean her house, or feed her children. She couldn't communicate with friends who came to comfort her. She found it impossible even to pray.

How could this happen to Esther? Shouldn't knowing the facts about God keep a believer from collapsing, even under intense emotional stress? Shouldn't we have absolute, unruffled serenity of heart, no matter what happens?

Not necessarily. Some days are stormy. When dark clouds loom and thunder booms, women get scared. Maybe right now you are in a turbulent time. A private grief is consuming your thoughts and causing turmoil.

1. Is a storm now breaking around you? Explain.

_____

_____

IT'S OKAY TO FEEL TROUBLED

Some of life's tempests are like hurricanes: huge, public, and sensational. Others are more private—a secret drain on your emotional resources. Is it a sin to feel troubled during a storm? The answer is no.

Several times in the Gospels, we are told that Jesus was troubled in His spirit. As a man, He had human emotions. As God, He could not sin (Hebrews 4:15). If Jesus ever had a troubled heart, then we can conclude that to feel upset is not sin.

A present storm

Jesus walked into a storm in the town of Bethany. When He saw what was happening there, His heart ached.

2. Read John 11:1–44. What had just happened?

_____

_____

3. What was Jesus' relationship to Lazarus and his sisters?

_____

4. When Jesus came to their home, He saw a classic scene of mourning. Who was there in addition to the family (verses 19, 31, 33)?

_____

_____

These were community mourners. The word used to describe their expressions of grief indicates that they were weeping in loud, mournful sobs and plaintive laments. They may have been paid, professional mourners.

5. How did Jesus react to their expressions of hopeless sorrow (verse 33)?

_____

_____

His "groaning," or sighing, was a sign of the agitation of His spirit. He did not wail in the same way the crowd did. Instead, verse 35 tells us He _____, expressed by a different word that means a quiet shedding of tears.

6. Why did the crowd think He was weeping (verses 36–37)?

_____

_____

7. Jesus knew that He was going to raise His friend from the dead. Why then do you think He wept?

_____

_____

An approaching storm

> Now is my soul troubled, and what shall I say? Father, save me from this hour; but for this cause came I unto this hour. (John 12:27)

8. What event is described in Isaiah 53:3–7?

_____

This prophecy was about to be fulfilled. Jesus knew what was ahead, and in His humanity, He was distressed.

9. Just before His arrest in the garden, He experienced emotional pain as He faced the physical and spiritual suffering of the cross. List the words and phrases in the Isaiah passage that describe the sufferings He knew were coming.

_____

_____

It's not a pleasant picture, is it? No wonder Jesus' spirit was troubled! But even before the storm of the cross, another sad event needed to take place, in fulfillment of prophecy. Jesus in His humanity anticipated its coming and was "troubled in spirit."

10. Read John 13:21–27. What was the incident?

_____

11. Has a trusted friend ever betrayed you?

_____

Why was that betrayal so painful?

_____

_____

How did you respond?

_____

_____

When you talk to Jesus about it, can He understand? Explain.

_____

_____

Following this scene, Jesus retreated with His disciples to Gethsemane to talk to His Father. Read Matthew 26:36–46.

12. Write out the words from verses 37–38 that describe His emotions.

_____

_____

13. His heart was in such agony that two unusual events took place. What are they according to Luke 22:43–44?

_____

_____

14. The Bible could not make it any clearer. During a storm, or when one approaches, it's normal—not sinful—to feel troubled. Look up the word *stoic* in a dictionary. Write the definition here.

_____

_____

Our family once lived in the Tennessee countryside, where our nearest neighbors were cows. Those cows didn't go to the barn for shelter, even during fierce summer thunderstorms. They stood in the open pasture, placidly chewing their cud, ignoring thunder, wind, rain, and hail. Not even close lightning strikes sent them to shelter. I wondered at them and even envied their calmness. They really shouldn't have ignored the lightning. Sometimes, a day or two after a big thunderstorm, we'd smell an awful stench and discover a dead cow lying outside the fence, waiting to be picked up by the dead-cow collector. A little bit of healthy fear might have saved those poor bovine lives.

A stoic in a storm? That's not supposed to be you! Emotions are a gift of God for your good. Without joy, life would be boring. Without love, it would be lonely. Without fear, you would do reckless, dangerous things! And when tears come, God sees and understands them.

15. What do the following verses say about God and tears?

Psalm 56:8

_____

2 Kings 20:5

_____

Revelation 21:4

_____

IT'S OKAY TO ASK FOR RELIEF

Read 2 Corinthians 12:7–10. Paul learned to "take pleasure in infirmities, in reproaches, in necessities, in persecutions, in distresses for Christ's sake."

16. But first, what did he do (verse 8)?

_____

_____

In the story of Jesus praying in the garden (Matthew 26:36–46) we see that He prayed three times for deliverance from the coming pain of the cross.

17. What exact words did He use (26:39)?

_____

_____

18. When you're in a storm, is it sinful to feel troubled? Explain.

_____

_____

_____

19. Is it wrong to pray for deliverance? Explain.

_____

_____

IT'S NOT OKAY TO WORRY

Don't feel guilty for having upset emotions during life's storms. But do feel guilty if a crisis causes you to worry. Worry is not an emotion. It is a thought process—a process that you can, and must, control because worry is sin.

What is worry? How do you recognize it? How can you tell the difference between worrying and just thinking through a problem? Disciplined thought moves in a straight line through a tangle of difficulties to possible solutions. Worry is a swirling tornado of thoughts centered on a fear. They repeat themselves over and over, making you dizzy but accomplishing nothing else. When fretful thoughts begin to sound familiar, that's worry.

When you worry, you disobey God's commands. Acknowledge worry as a sin.

20. Paraphrase these verses as God's directions to you.

Psalm 37:1, 7

_____

_____

_____

Matthew 6:25–34

_____

_____

_____

21. What words does the Bible use in these verses for our modern word _worry?_

_____

_____

What are you specifically told not to worry about?

_____

What have you been worrying about lately?

_____

_____

Is your worry on this list?

_____

When you worry, you show distrust in the truthfulness of God.

22. What phrase in Titus 1:2 assures you that God is always truthful?

_____

_____

23. According to 1 John 5:10, when you don't believe what God says, what are you actually doing?

_____

Would you be willing to openly call God a liar? When you tolerate worry, you are showing that you do not believe He tells the truth. Worry accuses God of making false promises.

In Philippians 4:19 Paul promises, "My God shall supply all your need according to his riches in glory." A worrier responds, "You forgot one!" The writer of Hebrews says in 13:5, "He hath said, I will never leave thee, nor forsake thee." A worrier responds, "You've forgotten me, God!" First Peter 5:6–7 says, "Humble yourselves therefore under the mighty hand of God . . . casting all your care upon him; for he careth for you." A worrier responds, "It's up to me to take care of my problems. Nobody else is going to do it." Romans 8:28 promises that "all things work together for good to them that love God, to them who are the called according to his purpose." A worrier declares, "My circumstances are intolerable—a miserable mess." Worry lies. Don't believe its lies!

When you worry, you harm God's temple.

Think how indignant you feel when a vandal maliciously damages a church building. But God does not dwell in a building the way He once dwelt in the tabernacle or temple.

24. Where is His temple now—His dwelling place on earth (1 Corinthians 6:19)?

_____

His temple should be kept clean and healthy, worthy to be the dwelling place of the Holy Spirit. It does not belong to you. It is held as a stewardship; it actually belongs to God. Worry causes emotional stress that can lead to physical illness. This vandalizes the temple, and that dishonors the Lord, Who lives there.

THERE IS A WAY TO STOP WORRYING

25. Write out Philippians 4:6–7.

_____

_____

_____

_____

_____

_____

_____

26. According to these two verses, what are you permitted to be anxious, fretful, or worried about?

_____

Instead, what are you supposed to do?

_____

And what will be the result?

_____

The word *keep* in verse 7 is very interesting. It is a military term depicting a sentinel guarding a camp or castle. When you refuse to worry, and instead pray and thank God, your mind will be guarded from attacks of fear and panic. You won't "go to pieces" when trouble comes—as it surely will.

You don't have to worry, no matter what happens. Even in a storm, Jesus Christ is with you. He controls the tempests, and He will keep His beloved child safe.

The next time a storm breaks, discipline your mind to obey Philippians 4:6–7. You will be amazed at the peace in your heart.

Lesson 4 # A Sweet Heart

Sweetheart—Honey—Sugar Pie—these are nicknames for people we love. Names like Sourpuss aren't nearly as flattering! We naturally enjoy sweetness and detest bitterness.

Are you sweet? God wants you to have a sweet heart. Your life, sacrificed to Him, can offer a sweet savor for His enjoyment.

A SWEET SAVOR

God is a spirit and does not have a body like man. But so that we can more easily comprehend all He is, the Bible describes God in human terms. God has no literal, physical

- ears, but we're told that the Lord's ear is not "heavy, that it cannot hear" (Isaiah 59:1).

- eyes, but still the "eyes of the Lord are in every place, beholding the evil and the good" (Proverbs 15:3).

- hands, yet the heavens are the "work of [His] fingers" (Psalm 8:3).

- nose, yet the aroma connected with certain sacrifices is to Him "a sweet savor" (Genesis 8:21).

Old Testament sacrifices

God is said to have smelled the aroma—the sweet savor—produced by sacrificial offerings. The word *savor* is related to both smell and taste. (If you hold your nose while eating, food has no taste—a technique some of us learned in childhood while eating certain vegetables.)

1. Read Genesis 4:3–7. What two men brought sacrifices to God?

_____

_____

   What were their offerings?

_____

   Which sacrifice was accepted and which was rejected and why?

_____

_____

_____

_____

We don't know when or how God instructed Cain and Abel about acceptable sacrifices. But it is obvious that both knew God's rules and one did not obey them.

2. Genesis 8:20–22 is the first mention of smell in connection with God. What did God smell?

_____

   What did He promise in response?

_____

3. Where did the clean animals (the ones acceptable for sacrifice) come from? Find the answer in Genesis 7:1–3.

_____

_____

4. What does this tell us about God's plans and Noah's obedience?

_____

_____

God established the Jewish sacrificial system as an object lesson of the awfulness of sin, as a reminder of the need for purification from sin, as an illustration of the holy demands of God, and as a foreshadowing, or type, of the death of Christ.

5. When an "offering made by fire unto the Lord" was done God's way, what did He smell (Exodus 29:18)?

_____

The place, the time, the people, the method—these were all carefully specified by God. Notice the detailed instructions about the preparation of holy oil in Exodus 30:22–25.

6. What was prohibited in verses 31–33?

_____

_____

_____

Why would God give such painstakingly detailed guidelines for sacrifices? Was He just trying to make life more difficult for the children of Israel? Or did He have some other purpose in mind?

7. Find a clue in Genesis 6:22. What does God hope to see in His servants?

_____

_____

8. Read Leviticus 26:27–31. Why would the Lord allow judgment on His chosen people and "not smell the savor of their sweet odors" (verse 31)?

_____

_____

9. What four things did God say He would not do in Amos 5:21–27?

_____

_____

Why (verse 26)?

_____

_____

10. In Jeremiah 6:16–20, what does God say about

    their burnt offerings?

_____

    their sacrifices?

_____

    Why were these rejected?

_____

The sacrifice of the wicked is abomination: how much more, when he bringeth it with a wicked mind? (Proverbs 21:27)

11. What heart attitude makes a sacrifice unacceptable to God? Read Matthew 15:7–9 for Jesus' answer.

_____

12. In contrast, what attitude of heart makes a sacrifice "a sweet savor" to Him? What "smell" does He love?

_____

Hath the Lord as great delight in burnt offerings and sacrifices, as in obeying the voice of the Lord? Behold, to obey is better than sacrifice, and to hearken than the fat of rams. (1 Samuel 15:22)

New Testament sacrifice

The entire Jewish sacrificial system pointed to one coming event— the sacrifice of the perfect Lamb of God on the cross.

13. How did John the Baptist introduce Christ at His baptism (John 1:28–29)?

_____

_____

Animals sacrificed in the Old Testament had to be "without blemish" (Exodus 12:5).

14. How is Christ described in 1 Peter 1:19?

_____

15. Read Leviticus 17:11 and Hebrews 9:22. What was the one essential ingredient in any sacrifice for it to atone for sin?

_____

16. What price was paid for our redemption, according to 1 Peter 1:18–19?

_____

_____

17. Read Philippians 2:5–8. What phrase says that Christ went to the cross in obedience to His Father?

_____

_____

Christ always did His Father's will, but it wasn't always easy. He paid a great price to obey but He did! And at the moment of His death, when He cried, "It is finished," the sacrificial system was ended, and the debt for our sin was paid in full.

18. What "smell" ascended to the Father at that moment (Ephesians 5:2)?

_____

Our sacrifices

Since Christ has died as our sacrificial Lamb, we no longer have to bring lambs or rams or any other physical sacrifice to the Lord. The sweet savor offering we bring to Him now is our obedience. We are sweet to Him only when we are obedient. Discover the sacrifices of obedience God longs for.

Not all Old Testament sacrifices were made in payment for sin. The peace offering, described in Leviticus 3, was brought voluntarily as an expression of gratitude for blessing. It was a symbol of peace and fellowship with God.

19. When this sacrifice was burned on the wood of the altar, what ascended to God (verse 5)?

_____

We offer this same "sweet savor" to God when we praise Him!

20. Underline the sacrifices mentioned in these verses.

Let us offer the sacrifice of praise to God continually, that is, the fruit of our lips giving thanks to his name. (Hebrews 13:15)

I will offer to thee the sacrifice of thanksgiving, and will call upon the name of the Lord. (Psalm 116:17)

It's odd to think of praise and thanksgiving as a sacrifice. You can understand this concept better by considering the command of Ephesians 5:20.

21. When and for what are we to give thanks?

_____

Is giving thanks always easy and natural? Is it sometimes very difficult? When you give thanks because it's right, not because you feel like it, that's a sacrifice of obedience. You are sacrificing your "right" to complain—your natural inclination to say just how you feel or how resentful you are that things haven't gone your way. You are doing what is supernatural rather than what is natural. This kind of obedience is better than any animal sacrifice.

I will praise the name of God with a song, and will magnify him with thanksgiving. This also shall please the Lord better than an ox or bullock that hath horns and hoofs. (Psalm 69:30–31)

22. What absolute, unconditional command are we given in the following verses: John 13:34; John 15:12; 1 John 3:11, 23?

_____

Is loving always easy and natural? Is it sometimes very difficult? When you love others even when you don't feel like it and they don't deserve it, that's a sacrifice. You are sacrificing your emotions—your fleshly desire to hate, to dislike, to despise people who are irritating, annoying, and mean! We are commanded to love, and when we obey that command, we are offering Him an acceptable sacrifice.

23. According to 1 John 3:16 and Ephesians 5:2, in what way will you then be imitating Jesus Christ?

_____

_____

Now thanks be unto God, which always causeth us to triumph in Christ, and maketh manifest the savour of his knowledge by us in every place. For we are unto God a sweet savour of Christ, in them that are saved, and in them that perish: to the one we are the savour of death unto death; and to the other the savour of life unto life. And who is sufficient for these things? (2 Corinthians 2:14–16)

These verses compare telling others about the Savior to spreading the sweet aroma of perfume.

24. Who "makes manifest" (diffuses, spreads) this fragrance through us?

_____

Where does He spread it?

_____

What two groups smell this sweet gospel fragrance?

_____

How do these groups respond? Are their reactions different?

_____

_____

When a Roman general returned home after battle, he would show off his plunder and his captives in a victory parade. Along the parade route, incense burned in censers and flowers were crushed under the horses' hooves. The strong, sweet odors brought joy to the victors' hearts but anguish to the enslaved and defeated.

Your witness of the good news will often be received as a sweet life-giving message. To others, however, the gospel is bad news—repulsive, like an odor of death. John 3:19 explains why: "Men loved darkness rather than light, because their deeds were evil." But still we are commanded to "preach the gospel to every creature" (Mark 16:15).

The word for _witness_ in the New Testament has the root meaning "martyr." In Acts 22:20 the word describing Stephen and translated "martyr" is the same word translated "witness" in Acts 1:8.

25. In what way can witnessing seem a kind of martyrdom?

_____

_____

Is witnessing always easy and natural? Is it sometimes very difficult? When you witness even when you don't feel like it, and when your testimony is rejected, that's a sacrifice. What are you sacrificing when you witness in obedience to God?

The Lord asks for just one more small sacrifice from you—it's your self!

Let's look carefully at Romans 12:1. Understand this verse and make it your own.

> _I beseech [beg] you therefore [because of all the truths just taught], brethren [fellow believers] by the mercies of God [because of God's compassionate_

kindness], that ye present [offer] your bodies a living sacrifice [not dead like Old Testament sacrifices], holy [pure, sanctified], acceptable unto God, which is your reasonable service [your logical, rational, intelligent response to the sacrifice He has made for you].

What's your heart's sweetness quotient? If you are a sourpuss rather than a sweetie pie, search His Word for areas of disobedience in your life.

You may discover a sin not confessed, a command not obeyed, or a will not surrendered. Ask for cleansing and for strength to obey. The Lord will hear and answer, and He will enjoy the sweet savor of your obedient heart!

Is your all on the altar of sacrifice laid?
Your heart, does the Spirit control?
You can only be blest,
And have peace and sweet rest,
As you yield Him your body and soul.
(Elisha A. Hoffman)

When you give yourself to God, you're not giving Him a fabulous gift. The Bible says that in you, "that is, in [your] flesh, dwelleth no good thing" (Romans 7:18). But when you offer yourself to Him, He will take your naturally sour heart and transform you into a sweet blessing.

Perfumes are made from natural and synthetic scents blended with bases that anchor the fragrance and give it longevity. Some of these bases are otherwise useless, nauseating substances such as ambergris, a greasy mass found in the intestines of sick whales.

Perfumers take such disgusting, rotten-smelling substances and through their skill transform them into a desirable, appealing product. Just like God, they make something sweet from awful raw ingredients.

Though as sinners, all you and I deserve is hell, "there is . . . no condemnation to them which are in Christ Jesus" (Romans 8:1). When you give yourself to Him, He will make you a sweet savor sacrifice, pleasing to Him. All He asks is your obedience. How sweet are you?

Lesson 5 A Servant's Heart

What did you want to be when you grew up? Most likely, your ambition was not to become a slave. Even now, you'd probably rather have a maid than be one! But the Bible summons you to servanthood. The goal of every Christian ought to be the same as Jesus Christ's—"not to be ministered unto, but to minister" (Matthew 20:28).

It's usually not fun to serve. Normally it's just plain old hard work, a discipline of obedience. But serving God and others from the heart with godly motives brings joy and blessings unique to those who serve. Even if you didn't grow up to be what you'd planned to be, it's not too late to pursue the greatest vocation of all—a servant!

> *Only fear the Lord, and serve him in truth with all your heart: for consider how great things he hath done for you. (1 Samuel 12:24)*

WHOM DO YOU SERVE?

1. In the following verses, underline whom you serve.

> *Not with eyeservice, as menpleasers; but as the servants of Christ, doing the will of God from the heart. (Ephesians 6:6)*

> *Serve the Lord with fear, and rejoice with trembling. (Psalm 2:11)*

Now therefore fear the Lord, and serve him in sincerity and in truth: and put away the gods which your fathers served on the other side of the flood, and in Egypt; and serve ye the Lord. (Joshua 24:14)

How much more shall the blood of Christ, who through the eternal Spirit offered himself without spot to God, purge your conscience from dead works to serve the living God? (Hebrews 9:14)

2. List some ways you are presently serving the Lord.

   _____

   _____

   _____

Look at your list. Do you see that serving the Lord always requires serving people? You can worship the Lord alone, but you cannot serve Him in solitude.

> **SERVING THE LORD = SERVING PEOPLE**

Serving the servants of the Lord

After the Lord gave the child Samuel to Hannah, she "lent him to the Lord" to be His lifelong servant. Samuel went to live at the temple with Eli, the high priest. First Samuel 2:11 says that this boy, around age twelve, "did minister unto [serve; wait on] the Lord before Eli the priest."

3. What services did he perform for Eli (1 Samuel 3:3–6, 15)?

   _____

   _____

These were simple, practical acts, but in doing them, Samuel was serving the Lord.

4. Read Luke 8:1–3. What were Jesus and His disciples doing?

   _____

   _____

What women were traveling with them?

_____

_____

What needs did they meet with their own resources?

_____

_____

This was the first ladies' missionary society!

Serving the saints of the Lord
The early church honored and financially supported older widows who had no other resources if they were devoted to serving the Lord and the church.

5. List the good works these women did (1 Timothy 5:10).

_____

_____

_____

These are all unglamorous, private acts of ministry to others, but they were done as service to the Lord.

6. Dorcas was a servant to the church (Acts 9:36–39) who met the needs of the poor. Verse 36 says she was "full of _____ and _____."

Specifically, what had she done and for whom?

_____

_____

What tools, then, did she use to serve the Lord?

_____

_____

7. Read the account of the judgment of the Gentiles in Matthew 25:34–40. What principle is being taught?

_____

_____

_____

As we have therefore opportunity, let us do good unto all men, especially unto them who are of the household of faith. (Galatians 6:10)

The opportunity to do good works = the obligation to do good works—to everyone, but especially to whom? Who is that?

For God is not unrighteous to forget your work and labour of love, which ye have shewed toward his name, in that ye have ministered to the saints, and do minister. (Hebrews 6:10)

The ministry of those who served the saints (poor, persecuted church members) is described here as a "work and labour [wearying, painful toil] of love," done in the name of God.

8. In contrast, what does 1 John 3:17 say about a Christian who does not meet the physical needs of other believers?

_____

_____

9. Read Romans 12:13, 1 Peter 4:9, and Hebrews 13:2. What is one practical way to love and serve?

_____

When you do this, what tools are you using to serve the Lord?

_____

_____

How Do You Serve?

Only fear the Lord, and serve him in truth with all your heart: for consider how great things he hath done for you. (1 Samuel 12:24)

10. How do you recognize service that's done from the heart? What does service that's not from the heart look like? (Remember the Bible definition of *heart*—your emotional, mental, and spiritual self.)

_____

_____

11. According to this verse, what should you keep in mind as you serve?

_____

_____

12. What emotions should accompany your service (Psalm 100:2; Romans 12:11)?

_____

_____

What "great things" has God done for you? Have you been serving Him grudgingly, motivated by guilt and obligation, or in jubilant response to His blessings?

Your physical body is your tool for service. Though you love and worship God spiritually, service always involves action.

13. Every woman is allowed to choose whose servant she will be. Read Romans 6:13–23 and give the two options you have—and their outcomes. (Your "members" are your body parts.)

_____

_____

_____

14. Your choice of whom you serve with your body stems from a spiritual decision you have made (or not made). What surrender does Romans 12:1 beg you to make?

_____

_____

15. Read 1 Corinthians 6:19–20. What amazing truth about the Holy Spirit is taught in verse 19?

_____

_____

Therefore, you are not _____.

So, what is your obligation?

_____

_____

16. How have you used your body to serve others this week? If you are not using your body to serve others, what does that say about your spirit?

_____

_____

Why Do You Serve?

Every Christian has received at least one spiritual gift. You (yes, you!) have something special to contribute to the body of Christ.

> *But unto every one of us is given grace according to the measure of the gift of Christ. (Ephesians 4:7)*

> *But every man hath his proper gift of God, one after this manner, and another after that. (1 Corinthians 7:7)*

> *But the manifestation of the Spirit is given to every man to profit withal. (1 Corinthians 12:7)*

> *But all these worketh that one and the selfsame Spirit, dividing to every man severally as he will. (1 Corinthians 12:11)*

17. Ephesians 4:12–16 tells how the body of Christ will gain when believers exercise their spiritual gifts. List those benefits.

_____

_____

_____

18. According to 1 Corinthians 13:1–3, what one trait is absolutely essential if any spiritual gift is to benefit others?

_____

Love is always focused on others, not on self. You don't receive a spiritual gift so that you can be proud of it or enjoy it by yourself but so that you can use it to serve the church.

19. Romans 12:3–10 compares the body of believers to a physical body, in which all members (all parts) have been gifted for their office (the role they are to play).

Where did your gift come from (verse 3)?

_____

How should that affect your attitude toward your gift?

_____

Do we all have the same gifts (verses 4, 6)?

_____

What is our relationship to Christ and to each other (verse 5)?

_____

What seven spiritual gifts are named (verses 6–8)?

_____

_____

_____

With what kind of love are you to serve (verse 9a)?

_____

In what practical way do you show love (verse 10)?

_____

Notice how all these ways of serving are focused on people. Do you recognize any of these gifts as yours? Are you using them?

My husband and I were visiting in the home of a couple who had been members of our church. Explaining why they had recently decided to join another, much larger church, the wife said, "Well, it's just like shopping. If K-Mart doesn't have what you want, you go to Wal-Mart instead."

Based on what you have just learned, what's wrong with that sort of consumer mentality toward the local church? Is it biblical for a Christian to choose a church based on what it offers her? Or does she have other obligations to the body?

First Corinthians 12 gives another comparison of the body of Christ with a physical body.

20. Why did the Lord make His children (the parts of His body) different from each other (verses 14–20)?

_____

_____

_____

Is any member of the body unimportant, unnecessary, insignificant, or inferior? Explain (verses 21–24).

_____

_____

Instead of being divided, how should we respond to each other (verses 25–26)?

_____

We serve each other in the body by recognizing the value of every person's spiritual gift and by sharing joys and giving emotional support in trials. Don't fret about identifying your spiritual gift. Just tell the Lord you will serve Him by serving others and then watch for doors to open. Walk through them, and you'll soon sense what you do best.

Peter sums up our topic in 1 Peter 4:10–11. He says that you are to minister to others the gift you have received, because you are simply the steward, not the owner, of your gift.

21. If you have a speaking gift, how are you to speak?

_____

If you have a serving gift, how are you to serve?

_____

What's your ultimate goal for using your gift?

_____

Ruth serves the Lord by playing the piano and teaching children in her church in spite of crippling arthritis and other painful ailments. When I asked her how she does it, she answered, "I don't know. I just know that I'm supposed to serve the Lord and that when I try, He helps me. Every time I play the piano, He gets the glory, because everybody knows I can't play with hands like these!"

22. What was Isaiah's honest appraisal of himself (Isaiah 6:5–8)?

_____

_____

What did God do for Isaiah?

_____

_____

What was Isaiah's immediate response?

_____

_____

Simon the Pharisee thought he was righteous, but he omitted some simple acts of service to Jesus (Luke 7:36–48).

23. What were they (verses 44–46)?

_____

_____

Why did the sinful woman do much more (verse 47)?

_____

_____

According to Jesus, who will love and serve the Lord most?

_____

_____

Jesus Christ came to earth as a servant, not as a King; as a man, not in His glory as God.

24. Read Philippians 2:5–8. What was Jesus' ultimate act of service?

_____

Even before His death, He set an example of servanthood. Read John 13:3–15.

25. What simple, humble service did He do for His disciples?

_____

Why did He do that? Was it just because their feet were dirty?

_____

_____

What example was He setting for His disciples (and you)?

_____

_____

In Mark 10:35–45. Jesus' disciples were competing for dominance in His kingdom. Jesus told them, "Whosoever will be great among you, shall be your minister: and whosoever of you will be the chiefest, shall be servant of all."

If you were asked to serve in a president's cabinet, you'd be honored. But you have an infinitely greater privilege—to serve the King of Kings! You serve Him by serving His people. God makes a promise to you, His servant, in Hebrews 6:10: "God is not unrighteous to forget your work and labour of love."

But I am among you as he that serveth. (Luke 22:27)

"Once we realize that Jesus has served us even to the depths of our meagerness, our selfishness, and our sin, nothing we encounter from others will be able to exhaust our determination to serve others for His sake." (Oswald Chambers)

Lesson 6 A Forgiving Heart

Thousands of lawsuits are filed every day. Mates, neighbors, and relatives seek revenge for real or imagined wrongs. These battles rarely lead to any sort of peaceful reconciliation. Instead, they leave behind lasting scars and bitterness.

Not all conflicts end up in the courtroom, of course. Most simmer for years in homes, neighborhoods, offices, and churches; often the people involved end up in doctors' offices with physical or emotional disorders. Physicians prescribe tranquilizers and antidepressants as remedies for a sickness that is actually spiritual—the sickness of unforgiveness.

Few people are willing to admit fault and accept blame, choosing rather to shift blame, representing themselves as victims. Fewer still understand their responsibility to actively seek reconciliation with an offender. So conflicts aren't resolved. Simple arguments escalate into private wars.

Even believers are subject to this disease of unforgiveness. Are you? Examine yourself honestly. Are you harboring unforgiveness? Do you believe it's justified? If so, watch out. There's a bitter weed growing in your heart, and it will defile you and those closest to you. It's time to face it as a sin and eradicate it!

WHY MUST YOU FORGIVE?
There will always be something to forgive
You live on earth with other sinners, and they will sin against you. They will lie about you, cheat you, and reject you. Friends will act like enemies, and enemies will act like the Devil. Prepare yourself. It will come!

1. Jesus warned His disciples in Matthew 5:10–12 that suffering would come. What forms of suffering did He predict for His followers?

_____

_____

_____

2. Paul told the Philippian church that the ministry they were given (granted as a favor from God) was not only to believe on Him but also to do what (Philippians 1:29)?

_____

3. Paul understood what their suffering would mean. List the painful experiences he and the other apostles were enduring, according to 1 Corinthians 4:9–13.

_____

_____

_____

_____

4. It sounds awful! But whose will (verse 9) was it for the apostles to be a theater (a spectacle) to the world as the scum of the earth?

_____

5. Should you expect a trouble-free life because you are a Christian?

_____

Forgiveness is a command

Your parents may have had you memorize Ephesians 4:32 as a child, but "be ye kind one to another, tenderhearted, forgiving one another . . ." is just as much a command to adults as to children. Notice the connection God makes between a tender heart and a forgiving spirit.

6. How does the condition of your *heart* affect your willingness to *forgive*?

_____

_____

This command is repeated in Colossians 3:13.

7. To whom is it directed (verse 12)?

_____

What six character traits are listed before and after the command (verses 12, 14)?

_____

_____

Compare this list to Galatians 5:22–26.

8. What can you conclude about forgiveness? Is forgiving an easy, natural, human act? If not, how can you possibly obey the command to forgive?

_____

_____

_____

Forgiving is a condition of your own forgiveness

When you repeat the Lord's Prayer, as recorded in Matthew 6, you may recite verse 12 without thinking: "And forgive us our debts, as we forgive our debtors." But right after the "amen" of the prayer, in verses 14–15, the Lord restates this statement as a warning.

9. Copy this warning.

_____

_____

_____

_____

_____

WHAT IS FORGIVENESS?

Forgiveness is not a feeling. It is a duty. It is an action you take, whether you feel like it or not, because you want to obey God. Remember—He has chosen to forgive you!

10. Underline the phrases in the following three verses that teach that God's forgiveness is His determined decision—His resolution.

   I, even I, am he that blotteth out thy transgressions for mine own sake, and will not remember thy sins. (Isaiah 43:25)

   For I will forgive their iniquity, and I will remember their sin no more. (Jeremiah 31:34)

   And their sins and iniquities will I remember no more. (Hebrews 10:17)

How can an omniscient God (One Who knows everything) forget? His "forgetting" is not accidental. It's deliberate. He chooses not to remember. He will never again charge you with your forgiven sins; He will never use them against you. God has buried your forgiven sins in the depths of the sea (Micah 7:19). He knows where they are, but He will never retrieve them. That is His choice.

Angel, our much-loved dog, died on a rainy winter evening. My husband and son buried her at the base of a tree in our Tennessee backyard. When we moved a year later, we left her bones there. We hadn't forgotten her or the place where she was buried (we still haven't), but we had no interest in digging up her bones and taking them with us.

You, too, can choose to forgive, to bury old bones of bitterness you have been carrying as a weapon for beating your enemy on the head! Forgiveness is a choice—a godly choice.

WHEN ARE YOU TO FORGIVE?

Again, we look to God as our example of forgiveness.

11. When does He forgive? Find the answer in the following verses.

1 John 1:9

_____

2 Chronicles 7:14

_____

Psalm 86:5

_____

12. Summarize these conditions in a few words. Before you can be forgiven, you must

_____

The forgiveness of sins is a two-way transaction. You *ask*. God *forgives*.

What about forgiveness in human relationships?

13. Find two "if-then" statements in Luke 17:3:

If your brother_____ against you, then
_____ him.

If your brother _____, then
_____ him.

It's another two-way transaction. He *asks*. You *forgive*.

God doesn't forgive without our repentance. You give forgiveness when the other person repents too. But there's more—keep on reading!

Look back at the first "if-then" of Luke 17:3. Your responsibility to your offender is to point out his wrongdoing—not as an angry, hostile attack but as an honest, loving, persistent effort to bring him to repentance so forgiveness can take place.

14. Matthew 18 contains a simple plan to follow when you have been wronged by another believer. Write out the steps.

Step 1 (verse 15)

_____

Step 2 (verse 16)

_____

Step 3 (verse 17)

_____

Step 4 (verse 17)

_____

Is this the pattern that Christian women usually follow when they are offended? Instead they often get angry, gossip, and slander the offender—which makes the conflict worse.

15. What is the purpose of this process in Matthew 18 (verse 15)?

_____

_____

Usually, a calm, private conversation settles the whole conflict quickly. In fact, you'll often find that the offender had no idea she hurt you. She never intended that at all; she was simply careless. Or if she did know she wounded you, she is now sorry and glad for an opportunity to apologize.

16. Read 1 Peter 4:8. Why do you not need to make an issue of every small offense?

_____

_____

What if your enemy is not a believer? Then you shouldn't be surprised! The world does not love God's children.

Remember Jesus' words in John 15:18–19: "If the world hate you, ye know that it hated me before it hated you. If ye were of the world, the world would love his own: but because ye are not of the world, but I have chosen you out of the world, therefore the world hateth you."

17. List the seven principles of Romans 12:17–21 for dealing with unbelieving enemies.

_____

_____

_____

_____

_____

If you live by these principles, others may tell you you're a pushover, an easy target, or a fool! But our guidance comes from God, not from people. He is our model for how to treat enemies.

How does God treat His enemies?

18. Read Matthew 5:43–48. In the last verse, Jesus sets what lofty goal for His disciples?

_____

How does the Father treat His enemies (verse 45)?

_____

To be like Him, how are we to treat our enemies (verses 43–44)?

_____

Are you then free to ignore, insult, or belittle someone who has offended you, just because she is unrepentant?

_____

19. In practical terms, how are you supposed to treat your enemy?

_____

_____

_____

WHAT HAPPENS IF YOU DON'T FORGIVE?

You damage your own relationship with God

Unforgiveness destroys friendships. Indulge it often enough, and you'll end up as an isolated, lonely old woman. But the damage unforgiveness does to your relationship with God is even more devastating.

Unforgiveness hinders your prayer life.

20. How does God respond to the prayers of a woman who knows there is sin in her heart and is not willing to repent (Psalm 66:18)?

_____

_____

Think about a person who has hurt you. What was her sin?

21. If you don't forgive, what is your sin?

_____

Read James 2:10. Which sin is worse—yours or hers? Why?

_____

_____

22. Write in your own words the Lord's instructions in Mark 11:25.

_____

_____

_____

Unforgiveness hinders your Christian service.

Matthew 5:23–24 explains, "Therefore if thou bring thy gift to the altar, and there rememberest that thy brother hath ought against thee; leave there thy gift before the altar, and go thy way; first be reconciled to thy brother, and then come and offer thy gift."

23. Bringing a sacrifice to the temple was a public act of worship. List some of these public acts in your church.

_____

_____

24. If you know that someone believes you have offended her, what are you supposed to do (notice who takes the initiative to resolve the conflict)?

_____

_____

You put yourself in bondage

Forgiveness frees; bitterness makes you its slave. The person you have not forgiven becomes a heavy weight chained to your leg. You will drag him along all through your years, and then wonder why you're tired and miserable. It's time to break that chain!

Remember the story of Joseph? He had good reason to be angry with his brothers. They had kidnapped him, sold him into slavery in Egypt, and told his beloved father, Jacob, that he was dead. When his brothers finally appeared before him in Genesis 42, he was a powerful man in Pharaoh's court. He could have had vengeance on his abusers; but he didn't.

25. Why did Joseph not take vengeance (Genesis 50:18–20)?

_____

_____

Instead of getting even, what did Joseph do (Genesis 50:21)?

_____

_____

Because Joseph trusted God, he could forgive his brothers. Joseph was at one time in Pharaoh's prison. He refused to let himself be locked into the emotional prison of unforgiveness. Are you in that prison? What are you going to do about it?

What if someone claims to be sorry but then does the same thing again and again, and again? How many times do you have to forgive?

26. Read Matthew 18:21–22. Do you think the Lord meant for us to keep a tally, and to stop forgiving at offense 490? If not, what did He mean?

_____

_____

Read Psalm 103:3: "Who forgiveth _____ thine iniquities." That's our model to follow!

What if your bitterness is toward a person who is dead, so that there is no possibility of reconciliation?

Wherever that person is now, she knows she did wrong. Your focus ought not to be on your old enemy but on your own heart. Ask God for cleansing from bitterness. Give Him your emotional baggage. Ask Him to erase bad memories and to heal your wounded spirit.

Apply Philippians 3:13–14 and move on!

Brethren, I count not myself to have apprehended: but this one thing I do, forgetting those things which are behind, and reaching forth unto those things which are before, I press toward the mark for the prize of the high calling of God in Christ Jesus.

A forgiving heart is a heart that pleases God. Does the condition of your heart please Him?

A young woman was devastated when, soon after marriage, her husband announced that he did not want to have children, for her deep desire was to be a mother. After much struggle, she resolved to forgive her husband for his wrong of not telling her this decision before she said "I do."

When the Lord opened a door for her to teach kindergarten, she saw this as His way of easing her pain and satisfying her desire to mother children. For thirty years she joyfully taught five-year-olds.

A health problem then arose that required her to have medical tests, including a genetic study. While discussing the test results, a doctor asked her how many miscarriages she had had. "None," she replied. "My husband did not want to have children."

"You have a genetic defect," continued her doctor, "that would have prevented you from carrying a child full term. If you had ever become pregnant, you would have miscarried."

"Just think," she said after telling me her story, "I could have wasted all those years being bitter toward my husband for not giving me what the Lord never intended for me to have."

Lesson 7 A Protected Heart

Ribs protect the heart that pumps your blood, but the Bible protects the heart that is the real you: your spiritual, emotional, mental self. Just as ribs help you stay alive physically, the Bible is necessary to your spiritual survival. It reveals God and His truth. It shows you who you are and cleanses your heart. It keeps you on the right path and protects you from danger. The Bible is an indispensable book, for it keeps you from sin!

> _Thy word have I hid in mine heart, that I might not sin against thee. (Psalm 119:11)_

WHAT IS THE BIBLE?

The Bible is God's revelation of Himself

We will begin with two assumptions:

1. God is real.

2. You are His creature.

These two assumptions lead to two conclusions:

1. Because you are His creature, you are accountable to Him.

2. Because you are accountable to Him, you need to know what He expects of you.

God has not left you to reach your own conclusions about Him. He took the initiative to introduce Himself to you when He left you the Bible—a paper and ink document.

1. In what other ways could He have communicated His truth? Why do you think He chose a written record rather than some other means of communication?

_____

_____

_____

The Bible is God's inspired Word

Is this book God's genuine, unique revelation? That is probably the most important question in life. Let's discover what this book says about itself.

2. Read 2 Timothy 3:16–17 to find answers to these questions.

How was Scripture (literally "the writing") given?

_____

Inspired means "breathed." Who breathed it?

_____

Therefore, Who is the Bible's author?

_____

Second Peter 1:20–21 says, "No prophecy of the scriptures is of any private interpretation. For the prophecy came not in old time by the will of man: but holy men of God spake as they were moved by the Holy Ghost." The source of Bible truth was not "the will of man."

3. Which member of the Trinity gave "holy men of God" the words to write?

_____

Over 3800 times, the Bible claims that it is God's Word, not man's. God superintended godly, obedient men as they recorded His words without error, using their unique personalities, minds, and vocabularies. These writers consistently refer to the words they wrote as the authentic words of God.

The Bible is truth

4. Read John 17:17 to fill in the blank: _____ = TRUTH

   What then can you say about all books, philosophies, teachings, or even religions that contradict the Bible?

   _____

   _____

5. If the Bible isn't the inspired Word of God but makes this claim 3800 times, what can you conclude about the Bible?

   _____

   _____

6. But if it is true, what role should the Bible play in your daily life?

   _____

   _____

WHAT DOES THE BIBLE DO?

The Bible unambiguously claims to be God's inspired Word—the only source of truth. You will be personally persuaded of its power when you see what it can do for you. First Thessalonians 2:13 says that when you hear and receive the Bible "not as the word of men, but as it is in truth, the word of God," it will "effectually work" in you. Its words, through the power of its Author, will go to work in you, and you will never be the same!

The Bible reveals

7. Read Hebrews 4:12–13. What three adjectives describe the Word of God?

   _____

   _____

Does this sound like an obsolete, irrelevant book? No, it's as alive and powerful as its Author!

8. What does this razor-sharp sword do? It pierces, or penetrates, into your soul and spirit, to your "joints and marrow." And it discerns—detects and sees—the _____ and _____ of your heart. What are these?

_____

This may not be pleasant! But this exposure has a purpose—the revelation of the real you to "the eyes of him with whom we have to do." This phrase means that we are accountable to God; we must give reckoning to Him, now and in eternity.

> But be ye doers of the word, and not hearers only, deceiving your own selves. For if any be a hearer of the word, and not a doer, he is like unto a man beholding his natural face in a glass: for he beholdeth himself, and goeth his way, and straightway forgetteth what manner of man he was. But whoso looketh into the perfect law of liberty, and continueth therein, he being not a forgetful hearer, but a doer of the work, this man shall be blessed in his deed. (James 1:22–25)

9. What is the purpose of a mirror?

_____

_____

10. What would you say about someone who looks in the mirror, sees she looks a mess, and does nothing about it?

_____

_____

What about the woman who looks into the Word, sees her sin, but does nothing about it?

_____

_____

Can you recall a time when God's Word "read you" as you were reading it? What did you discover about your secret self? How did you respond to what you learned?

The Bible purifies

When you see your inner self reflected in God's mirror, you know you need to change. You might cry out, "How can I be different?" Where do troubled people go for help if they don't look to the Scriptures? Are they usually able to make a permanent change? Why or why not?

God's Word doesn't show you what is wrong with you and then leave you without help. Nor does it offer just a temporary fix for your problems. The Bible offers real, lasting change!

11. Write out John 17:17.

_____

_____

12. Read John 17:1–11. Who is speaking these words?

_____

To Whom is He speaking?

_____

About Whom is He speaking?

_____

13. Look up the word *sanctify* in a dictionary. What does it mean?

_____

_____

14. What is the only way to be sanctified, according to John 17:17?

_____

_____

15. Read Ephesians 5:25–27. Who loved the church?

_____

With what is He sanctifying and cleansing (purifying) the church?

_____

_____

Are you part of His church? If you are, what is His amazing, ultimate goal for you?

16. What tool does He use to accomplish this goal?

_____

_____

Are you letting Him use this tool consistently in your heart?

_____

For as the rain cometh down, and the snow from heaven, and returneth not thither, but watereth the earth, and maketh it bring forth and bud, that it may give seed to the sower, and bread to the eater: so shall my word be that goeth forth out of my mouth: it shall not return unto me void, but it shall accomplish that which I please, and it shall prosper in the thing whereto I sent it. (Isaiah 55:10–11)

17. What is the purpose of rain?

_____

You may not always immediately see what rain has accomplished, but that does not mean that its moisture was wasted. What promise does God make in Isaiah 55 about the water of His Word?

Have you ever read the Bible and then afterward thought, "I didn't get a thing out of that"? Is it possible for God's Word, when it's read carefully, to accomplish absolutely nothing?

In my kitchen, I wash fresh spinach in a colander under cold running water. The water runs over the leaves and out the holes. I don't always see the dirt and sand running off, but it's going down the drain nevertheless, leaving the spinach clean. I may not always discern its specific effect, but the Bible leaves me cleaner than it found me, as my heart is cleansed through "the washing of water by the word."

The Bible shows the way

Some paths of life seem smooth and attractive but are displeasing to God; others look rocky and difficult but are actually righteous roads. Your heart—mind, emotions, and spirit—will be easily misled unless you make the Bible your light. It will point out dangers and lead you in the right direction. It will keep you from stumbling or getting lost in a forest of wrong values.

Finding God's will is important. Jesus taught us to pray, "Thy will be done" (Matthew 6:10). Jesus Himself prayed, "Not my will, but thine be done" (Luke 22:42). In Ephesians 5:17, you're told not to be foolish but to understand "what the will of the Lord is."

18. Are you in a dark place right now, trying to decide between two paths, looking for His will? Where, according to Psalm 119:130, can you find light and wisdom?

_____

_____

Simply opening (entering) God's Word is the first step! Look for the precepts—general principles of right and wrong—that apply to your options. Often, the right way will be obvious immediately, because God's will never contradicts His written Word.

> ## HIS WORD = HIS WILL!

I delight to do thy will, O my God: yea, thy law is within my heart. (Psalm 40:8)

Then ask God for specific direction from Scripture. Many believers have found that a specific verse "comes alive" to them when they are reading prayerfully, asking the Lord to speak. Can you recall a time when this happened to you?

There may be danger within. Since you live in a dark world, you are always in danger of straying off the Lord's path into the gloom of sin.

19. What will daily exposure to the light of the Word do for you?

_____

Where does the Christian discover God's "way of life" (Proverbs 6:23)?

_____

How do you keep yourself from slipping, or wavering (Psalm 37:31)?

_____

A daily study of the Word is the secret of stability in your Christian walk.

With my whole heart have I sought thee: O let me not wander from thy commandments. (Psalm 119:10)

There may be danger without. Do you have enemies?

20. Every Christian has at least three enemies. Who are they?

1 Peter 5:8

_____

Romans 7:22–23

_____

1 John 2:16

_____

These are powerful foes! In your own strength, you'll be defeated as you battle them. But you don't have to fight them all by your weak little self!

21. How can you outsmart your enemies (Psalm 119:98)?

_____

_____

Jesus Christ used the Scriptures as a weapon to defeat the temptations of His enemy Satan (Matthew 4:1–11).

Above all, taking the shield of faith, wherewith ye shall be able to quench all the fiery darts of the wicked. And take the helmet of salvation, and the sword of the Spirit, which is the word of God. (Ephesians 6:16–17)

Thy word is a lamp unto my feet, and a light unto my path. (Psalm 119:105)

What would it be like to spend long winter evenings in a house without lights? What would you think of someone who lived in a house with lights but refused to turn them on?

Almost all the problems in the world are caused by ignorance or rejection of God's Word—all kinds of petty and serious crimes, abortion, homosexuality, divorce, greed, cheating, abuse, and much more.

22. Why do people refuse to turn on its lights? Find the answer in John 3:19–20.

_____

_____

23. Can you recall a time when you knew you should read the Bible but you just didn't want to? What was probably the reason for that?

_____

_____

My young son was doing a simple science project. He moistened a soft, fresh slice of bread and put it into a covered container in a dark closet. A week later, the bread that had been left in darkness was covered with mold. It was ugly and smelled of decay.

Do you have a sinful, ugly heart attitude? Does it stink to others and even to yourself? Maybe you're moldy! Daily exposure to the light of His Word will keep you fresh by preventing the decay of sin.

What Should You Do with the Bible?

Receive it eagerly

Paul and Silas once preached in the city of Berea, where the people responded to their message in a remarkable way. In Acts 17:11, the Bereans are called "more noble" than the Thessalonians because of the way they responded to God's Word. They received what they heard preached with "all readiness of mind." The word *readiness* means that they were eager, rushing forward, hungry for the truth. They didn't have to be coaxed or coerced into studying the Scriptures. The Bereans searched the Scriptures daily, not just on the Sabbath.

24. Read 1 Peter 2:2. What can you learn from the comparison made here about how you are supposed to receive God's Word?

_____

_____

Is Bible reading your chore or your delight? Just as a baby craves a mother's milk, a child of God longs for the nourishing Word.

Receive it meekly

25. According to James 1:21 what is the result of receiving the Word with meekness?

_____

_____

It must have been wonderful to sit on a hillside and hear Jesus teach. You were born too late for that! But today you have a personal Bible teacher, the Holy Spirit.

26. What things does He teach?

   1 Corinthians 2:9–13

_____

   John 14:26

_____

John 16:12–14

Blessed are they that hear the word of God, and keep it. (Luke 11:28)

Are you hearing the Word? Are you keeping it? Do you have a protected heart?

Lesson 8 A Speaking Heart

Have you ever heard words coming out of your mouth and been surprised by what you heard? Maybe your words were bitter and angry, harshly critical, or gossip disguised as chitchat. Or maybe they were unexpectedly sweet and peaceable! You might have wondered as you listened to yourself, "Where did that come from?"

God's Word helps us understand the source of our speech and teaches us how to make all our words pleasing to His ears.

THE SOURCE OF YOUR SPEECH

Where do words come from? The answer is in Luke 6:45:

> *A good man out of the good treasure of his heart bringeth forth that which is good; and an evil man out of the evil treasure of his heart bringeth forth that which is evil: for of the abundance of the heart his mouth speaketh.*

All your words come from your heart. They emerge as "good treasure" or "evil treasure," out of your heart's "abundance."

Words simply overflow from your heart and reveal the condition of your mental, emotional, and spiritual self. Every word that comes out of your mouth was first present in your heart.

Out of the abundance of the heart the mouth speaketh. (Matthew 12:34)

A SINFUL HEART → WICKED WORDS

Psalm 10 describes the wicked. The sinful man is proud, blasphemous and deceitful. Among other sins, "his mouth is full of cursing and deceit and fraud."

1. Where, according to Psalm 10:7, are his "mischief [trouble] and vanity [iniquity]" found?

_____

The wicked mouth is like the mouth of a venomous snake. Poison is in its throat, under the tongue, ready to be used. When an angry person wants to strike, toxic words are stored up, ready for use. Even a person whose mouth drips honey at other times can spew poison when provoked. You'll find similar descriptions of the wicked mouth in Job 20:12–14, Psalm 140:3, and Romans 3:13–14.

A RIGHTEOUS HEART → WISE WORDS

In contrast, words that please God and help others come from a heart that is right with God.

2. Proverbs 10:11; 18:4, and James 3:10–12 give us another vivid depiction of the source of speech. Describe the word picture that illustrates their truth.

_____

_____

THE IMPORTANCE OF YOUR SPEECH

3. Words have an enormous power for good or for evil. In fact, Proverbs 18:21 says that both _____ and _____ are in the power of your tongue. That's amazing influence!

4. In James 3:2–5, the tongue is compared to three familiar objects—three little things with great power. What are they?

_____

_____

Power for good

Good words make the speaker spiritually healthy.

> *Pleasant words are as an honeycomb, sweet to the soul, and health to the bones.* *(Proverbs 16:24)*

Pure, encouraging words restore healthy marrow to our spiritual "bones"—our spiritual vigor. Delightful, suitable, graceful, beautiful words strengthen and invigorate a famished spirit in the same way honey revives a weak, famished body.

5. Read Proverbs 12:18. What is the connection between mental and physical health? How do good and evil words affect your health? (Think about their effect on how you eat and sleep.)

_____

_____

_____

6. Read Proverbs 4:20–22. What promise is given to those who love the best words of all—God's words?

_____

_____

_____

_____

Good words feed others.

> *The lips of the righteous feed many: but fools die for want of wisdom.* *(Proverbs 10:21)*

7. What kinds of emotional and spiritual nourishment can good words provide for needy people?

_____

_____

8. Recall a time when you were fed by good words. Who spoke them and how did they affect you?

_____

_____

_____

Good words end conflicts.

9. Read Proverbs 15:1. Contrast the results of two kinds of words.

"Soft" (tender-hearted) words

_____

"Grievous" (hard-hearted, spiteful, harsh, bitter) words

_____

Recall the last battle you watched or took part in. What words "stirred up" the fight? What words could have ended it? A dispute is like a smoldering fire. Our words either douse the embers with water or stir them into flame. Do your words usually extinguish the fire or add fuel to it?

A wrathful man stirreth up strife: but he that is slow to anger appeaseth strife. (Proverbs 15:18)

Power for evil
Evil words cut.

10. To what sharp tools is the tongue compared?

Psalm 52:2

_____

Psalm 57:4

_____

Psalm 64:3

_____

11. A razor-sharp knife can be useful or deadly. Who determines how it's used?

_____

12. Give an example of "cutting" damage you have seen a tongue do.

_____

_____

_____

A wholesome [healing] tongue is a tree of life: but perverseness [viciousness] therein is a breach [a bruise, a crushing, a breaking] in the spirit. (Proverbs 15:4)

Think about today—yesterday—last week. Did your tongue produce healing and life, or did it bruise and crush?

Evil words destroy the speaker.

13. Read Proverbs 13:3. How do you recognize a person who "openeth wide his lips"?

_____

_____

14. In what ways is a woman who says everything she thinks (and some things she hasn't thought of yet) in danger?

Psalm 39:1

_____

Matthew 12:36–37

_____

Proverbs 10:19

_____

Ecclesiastes 5:3

_____

It is especially important to control your speech when you are among the wicked because evil words overheard by the wicked can harden them to truth or give them cause to blaspheme or mock truth.

THE COMMANDS FOR YOUR SPEECH

Ephesians 4:25–32 tells you how to speak in a way that pleases God and helps others. The rules are short and simple. You can obey them through the power of the Holy Spirit. When you do obey them, you will not "give place to the devil" (verse 27) or "grieve [cause sorrow to] the Holy Spirit" (verse 30). And you also do one other thing that everybody wants to do.

15. What is it according to Proverbs 21:23?

_____

_____

Let's look at two simple rules from Ephesians 4 that will keep you out of trouble. Before we do, recognize that biblical communication always requires speaking out loud. Every healthy physical body communicates with itself. The brain, through the nervous system, speaks to the rest of the body, and vice versa. If nerves are severed, communication stops, and the result is paralysis.

In a healthy marriage, a family, or a church, members communicate regularly and openly. There is no place for clamming up, pouting, sulking, or moping. God wants us to talk—really talk—to each other.

Rule #1—Speak the truth
16. What is truth?

_____

_____

What is a lie?

_____

_____

17. Who lies according to the following verses?

Psalm 58:3

_____

Colossians 3:8–10

_____

In heathen philosophy lying is an acceptable, normal, even necessary tool in life, for a pleasant lie "feels better" than a painful truth. If a lie is helpful and kind, we're told, then it is "right." Psalm 52:3 even says that the wicked love lying!

But the "new woman" will not lie no matter how useful it might be. Her words always reflect reality, not deceit. She hates lying, for she knows it displeases her Savior—and she values His approval over comfort, popularity, or gain.

God's Word teaches us never to lie, because lying damages His body.

18. Ephesians 4:25 says to put away [throw away]_____.
    Instead, we should speak _____ because
    _____.

19. What does this last phrase mean? Find the answer in Romans 12:5.

_____

_____

What would your physical life be like if parts of your body lied to each other? It would be uncoordinated chaos. You'd have unnecessary pain and would not be able to avoid danger. In the same way, untrue communication within the body of Christ causes pain and suffering.

It's essential for believers, members of His body, to always be truthful with each other.

God's Word teaches us never to lie, because lying causes us to imitate the wrong master.

20. How does John 8:44 describe the Devil?

_____

_____

And what does 1 Peter 2:22 say about Jesus Christ? (Compare the prophecy of the Messiah in Isaiah 53:9.)

_____

_____

When you lie, then you imitate _____, rather than Jesus Christ.

God's Word teaches us never to lie, because lying is repugnant to God.

These six things doth the Lord hate: yea, seven are an abomination unto him: a proud look, a lying tongue, and hands that shed innocent blood, an heart that deviseth wicked imaginations, feet that be swift in running to mischief, a false witness that speaketh lies, and he that soweth discord among brethren. (Proverbs 6:16–19)

21. Underline in the verses above the seven things the Lord hates [finds odious]. They are an abomination [abhorrent, disgusting] to Him. What is the only sin mentioned twice?

_____

God's word teaches us never to lie, because lying guarantees punishment.

22. Proverbs 19:5 and 9 name three of the sad outcomes a liar can expect. What are they?

_____

_____

The command to always speak truth does not give you permission to be brutally honest. It's not an excuse to heartlessly unload truth on someone with the attitude of "I just tell the truth; I don't care who it hurts." Ephesians 4:15 commands us to speak "the truth in love." That's *agape* love: self-sacrificial concern for the needs of others. Let's learn more about this kind of speech.

Rule #2—Speak to edify

Paul used the words *edify* and *edifying* about a dozen times in his epistles. They are architectural terms. An edifice is a building. A believer is like a building—a holy temple in the process of construction. You are not capable of building yourself alone; you need the help of other believers to be built up, or edified.

And your job, according to Ephesians 4:12, is to help other believers grow into perfect "buildings"—complete, fully Christlike—through your constructive contacts with them. Most of these contacts are verbal.

The first command in Ephesians 4:29 is not to let corrupt words out of your mouth.

23. List several synonyms for *corrupt*.

_____

_____

Profanity is one type of corrupt speech that violates the third commandment: "Thou shalt not take the name of the Lord thy God in vain [lightly, foolishly, irreverently]; for the Lord will not hold him guiltless that taketh his name in vain" (Exodus 20:7).

What do you think about the common exclamations, "Oh, my God" or "Oh Lord"? What about gee, golly, gosh, heck, and so forth? If you're not sure, look up these words in a dictionary.

24. Ephesians 4:31 lists more specific types of corrupt speech. List them and think about what they mean.

_____

_____

If you hear corrupt, foul, rotten speech coming out of your mouth, what does that tell you about your heart? Recall our look at Luke 6:45 at the beginning of this lesson.

Everybody gets angry sometimes. Irritation boils up inside in the shape of furious words until you just want to tell somebody off. She deserves it, and it would feel so good!

That's a fleshly response—to release your own pressure valve at the expense of another. You feel better, but she feels worse, so she then releases her own pressure valve right back at you. Clamor and corrupt words are flying. Nobody is built up. Nobody is helped.

There's a better way!

25. According to the second half of Ephesians 4:29, only what kinds of words are supposed to come out of your mouth?

_____

_____

Since our job is to help each other grow, sometimes it's necessary to talk about unpleasant issues. If you want to help another person spiritually, you might have to point out negatives. It is possible to correct in a positive, edifying way.

26. Write out some practical guidelines for a discussion like this. How can you communicate love, encouragement, and respect even when you are giving reproof? You'll find one idea in Galatians 6:1.

_____

_____

_____

But what if someone really deserves an angry rebuke? What if he's not even one bit sorry? The answer is at the end of Ephesians 4:29. Our edifying words will "minister grace to the hearers." What is grace? How can your words "minister grace"?

Are you having continual trouble with your tongue? Mouth trouble always starts in the heart (Luke 6:45 again). That's the place to start making your tongue pleasing to God.

Pray these Scriptures often and see what happens to your speech.

> *Let the words of my mouth, and the meditation of my heart, be acceptable in thy sight, O Lord, my strength, and my redeemer. (Psalm 19:14)*

Every woman with a mouth needs both strength and a Redeemer.

> *Set a watch, O Lord, before my mouth; keep the door of my lips. (Psalm 141:3)*

Only the Lord Himself is capable of guarding your tongue. But He can, and He will, make your words a sweet blessing.

> *Hear; for I will speak of excellent things; and the opening of my lips shall be right things. For my mouth shall speak truth; and wickedness is an abomination to my lips. All the words of my mouth are in righteousness; there is nothing froward or perverse in them. (Proverbs 8:6–8)*

Lesson 9 A Contented Heart

During His thirty-three years on earth, Jesus showed us how to live. One of the most striking features of His earthly life was its simplicity. He accumulated heavenly treasures, not earthly ones. He didn't waste His time; He invested it. He lived simply because He knew He was going to die.

Eternity is near us too. We know that, but still our houses are packed with excess stuff. We allow trivial activities to crowd essential ones out of our schedule. A woman can always find someone else to blame, but this is actually a personal, heart issue. A woman whose heart desires a simple life will find a way to achieve it.

In this lesson, you will discover what the Bible says about simplifying possessions. Christ set the example for us, and principles in His Word direct us toward a life of being contented with less.

THE EXAMPLE OF SIMPLICITY IN POSSESSIONS

Jesus Christ, the King of Kings and Lord of Lords, could have lived in great pomp and splendor on the earth; but He didn't. He lived and died a poor man—as an example for us.

1. What does Matthew 8:20 say about Jesus?

_____

_____

Because He had an earthly body, He needed to eat and sleep. He could have miraculously created shelter or food for Himself and His disciples, but He didn't.

2. How were His basic needs provided (Luke 8:1–3)?

_____

_____

It was humbling for Christ to need their help and a sign of His meekness that He accepted it.

3. Why did He willingly live in poverty (2 Corinthians 8:9)?

_____

_____

4. What kind of riches does He desire for us? Is it more "stuff"?

_____

_____

James cautioned his readers to beware of oppressing the poor because the poor were actually wealthy!

5. In what ways were they rich? What was their inheritance (James 2:5)?

_____

_____

Keeping in mind what you have just learned about Jesus, answer these questions:

6. Are material riches always a sign of God's blessing? Explain.

_____

_____

7. How do you know that a person can be both righteous and poor?

_____

_____

THE PRINCIPLES OF SIMPLICITY IN POSSESSIONS

Living by these scriptural principles requires living simply:

- The Contentment Principle

- The Priority Principle

- The Pilgrim Principle

- The Eternity Principle

The contentment principle

It's hard to be satisfied with what you already own. Maybe right now you are thinking, "If I just had _____, I'd be content!" It's easy to fall into the trap of believing that if you just get that one bigger, better, newer thing, then you'll be happy. Advertisers work hard to convince you of that.

8. The Bible, however, tells the truth in 1 Timothy 6:6–8. Write these verses in your own words.

_____

_____

_____

_____

_____

In this passage contentment is connected to godliness.

But godliness with contentment is great gain. (verse 6)

9. What is godliness?

_____

_____

What is contentment?

_____

_____

How are they linked?

_____

_____

_____

What does contentment in your heart say about your relationship with God?

_____

_____

A woman had recently moved to our area and was visiting our church. When I went to visit her in her new home, I was surprised by its size.

I asked, "Are you enjoying your new home?" The answer, I assumed, was obvious. What was not to like? It was more than adequate; it was luxurious—opulent—splendid!

But she frowned slightly as she answered, "Well, I really don't like it all that much." And then she proceeded to list its faults, all the appointments she felt it lacked.

I don't remember the rest of our conversation, but I do remember looking back at her mansion as I drove away and comprehending as never before that contentment has very little to do with a woman's surroundings and possessions. It has everything to do with the state of her heart.

Paul, a godly man, had learned contentment. Read his words in Philippians 4:10–14.

10. When was Paul content?

_____

Where did he get the capacity to be content even when in need?

_____

_____

What is your heart set on? Does it crave more stuff, or being like Him? Do you enjoy the "great gain" of godliness coupled with contentment?

Contentment comes from wanting only what God says you need.

> *For we brought nothing into this world, and it is certain we can carry nothing out. And having food and raiment [probably implies some sort of shelter as well as clothing] let us be therewith content. (1 Timothy 6:7–8)*

11. The day you were born, what did you own?

_____

What did you need to survive?

_____

Between birth and death, what is all we actually need?

_____

_____

12. Do you own anything that doesn't fit into the categories of food and shelter? If they're not necessities, what can we call them?

_____

Is it sinful to own more than the basics? No—it's a sign of God's exceeding goodness! What would you call an insistence that God provide more than your basic needs?

God calls His children to make a decision about possessions. Will you be content or will you seek to own more and more and more?

First Timothy 6:9–11 warns of the dangers of being discontent and greedy.

> *But they that will be [want to be, intend to be] rich fall into temptation and a snare, and into many foolish and hurtful lusts, which drown men in destruction and perdition. (verse 9)*

13. What sins are rooted in the desire to be rich?

_____

Underline the godly attributes mentioned in verse 11 below as being the result of *not* loving money (and the stuff it buys).

> *For the love of money is the root of all [sorts of] evil: which while some coveted after, they have erred from the faith, and pierced themselves through with many sorrows. But thou, O man of God, flee [escape, run away from] these things; and follow after [pursue] righteousness, godliness, faith, love, patience, meekness. (verses 10–11)*

Are you content with godliness? Is being godly enough to satisfy you? Are you insisting on having more than what God says you need?

The priority principle

The priority principle is found in Matthew 6:19–34. Read this passage carefully and then answer the following questions.

14. What are the two kinds of treasures (verses 19–20)?

_____

_____

Which are you told to gather?

_____

Why?

_____

_____

15. If your treasure is primarily on earth, what will you love and look to for happiness (verse 21)? (Remember that your heart is your emotional self.)

_____

_____

Where will you focus your thoughts? (Your heart is also your mental self.)

_____

_____

Where will you find your spiritual security? (Your heart is your spiritual self.)

_____

_____

Which makes you happier—buying new stuff or pleasing God?

Which do you think about more—improving your house or laying up treasure in heaven?

Where is your trust for the future—in a bank account, in a pension plan, or in your Father's provision?

16. Every woman must choose her master—someone or something to obey and serve. Who are the two contestants for the job (verses 22–24)?

   _____

   _____

   How do you know whether your master is God or mammon?

   _____

   _____

The priority principle is also stated clearly in Matthew 6:32–33 as a contrast between believers and Gentiles.

> *For after all these things [such as food and clothes] do the Gentiles [pagans, heathen] seek; for your heavenly Father knoweth that ye have need of all these things.*

In contrast, here's how believers are supposed to live.

But seek ye first the kingdom of God, and his righteousness and all these things shall be added unto you. (Matthew 6:33)

Notice how many times the words "all these things" appear in this passage.

17. Who puts priority on "all these things"?

   _____

   What should a Christian's priorities be?

   _____

   _____

In practical terms, how can you do this? You do need to work for some income, shop for groceries, and buy clothes—so how do you know if you are being obedient to the command of Matthew 6:33?

The mail comes, and in it is an unexpected check (it has been known to happen!). Maybe your tax refund is larger than expected or you've received an inheritance from a rich uncle. What is your first response to the extra income? Do you immediately plan what to buy? Or is your reaction a prayerful one: "How can I use this money to advance Your cause, Lord? What do You want me to do with this money?"

The pilgrim principle

18. Underline the two descriptive words for believers that are repeated in these verses.

   Dearly beloved, I beseech you as strangers and pilgrims, abstain from fleshly lusts, which war against the soul. (1 Peter 2:11)

   These all died in faith, not having received the promises, but having seen them afar off, and were persuaded of them, and embraced them, and confessed that they were strangers and pilgrims on the earth. (Hebrews 11:13)

Have you ever visited a new country, especially one with a different language from your own and very different customs? If so, you know what it means to be a "stranger," or foreigner. As a Christian, you do not actually belong to this world.

19. According to Philippians 3:20, where is your real home?

_____

This world is not your home, for you are already "risen with Christ." As a citizen of heaven, what should you love and value?

> *If ye then be risen with Christ, seek those things which are above. . . . Set your affection on things above, not on things on the earth. (Colossians 3:1–2)*

20. We all know about the *Mayflower* pilgrims. Why do we call them that? What does a pilgrim do?

_____

_____

_____

21. If you were going on a long hike (a pilgrimage), how would you pack your backpack?

_____

_____

If a Christian woman understands her role as a "stranger" and "pilgrim" on the earth, she will travel light! In practical terms, what will she do?

_____

_____

Our friends, an evangelist and his family, bought a new travel trailer. They loaded it with their belongings and began to travel in ministry. Within a short time, they were alarmed to see their new trailer coming apart at the seams. When they returned to the factory for repairs, a technician quickly found the problem: the trailer was overloaded. The weight of their possessions was more than the trailer could bear, so it had developed "stress fractures." These pilgrims could not travel and minister again until they had lightened their load.

The eternity principle

Christ taught the eternity principle in a parable, found in Luke
12:15–21. He began with the "moral of the story," found in verse 15.
Read the parable carefully.

22. Write the parable in your own words.

_____

_____

_____

_____

Why did God call the rich man a fool? Was it because he was rich? Was
it because he produced wealth and saved it?

Paul taught the eternity principle in 1 Corinthians 7:29–31.

23. Summarize his teaching.

_____

_____

_____

An elderly woman was excited about taking her first train trip. She
settled herself into her seat and began to arrange and rearrange her
bundles, lap robe, and pillow. Finally satisfied, she raised the window
shade to enjoy the passing scenery—just in time to hear the conduc-
tor announce her stop.

She bustled off the train muttering, "If I had known the trip was so
short, I wouldn't have wasted so much time getting comfortable!"

Long before Paul wrote 1 Corinthians, Solomon expressed the human
situation like this:

> As he came forth of his mother's womb, naked shall he return to go as he came,
> and shall take nothing of his labour, which he may carry away in his hand. And
> this also is a sore evil, that in all points as he came, so shall he go: and what profit
> hath he that hath laboured for the wind? (Ecclesiastes 5:15–16)

24. Which of your material possessions can you take with you into eternity?

In some religions, people have been buried with valuable goods because of a false belief that these would be of benefit in their "next life." When archaeologists have uncovered these tombs, those treasures are still there (if robbers haven't plundered them first). Nothing you own in this life can be taken with you into eternity.

Like all other "issues of life," contentment is a heart issue. Psalm 62:10 reminds you, "If riches increase, set not your heart upon them." Riches are too temporary, too distracting, and too unsettled for you to fix your heart and your hopes on them. Instead, hold your belongings in open hands, ready to give them back to God at any time.

Your brief life on earth is like a night spent in a hotel. All you really need in a hotel room are clean sheets and hot water. Maybe the Lord has provided for you an elegant hotel room with luxurious furnishings and fixtures. (Maybe, instead, your room is more like Motel 6!) In either case, God has promised that you will have all you need.

When it's time to check out of a hotel, do you cry at leaving the furniture behind? Of course not! You enjoyed it and took care of it while you were there. (You didn't carve your name on the dresser, did you?) But it wasn't hard to say goodbye to those furnishings because you knew all along that they were temporary. As a stranger and pilgrim, you were leaving in the morning for your real home.

Are you following Christ's example? Are you living a contented life?

Lesson 10 # A Rested Heart

SIMPLIFYING YOUR SCHEDULE

For thirty years, Jesus Christ lived on the earth without public recognition. After His baptism, He began three years of active ministry, calling and teaching disciples, feeding the hungry, healing the sick, and raising the dead. He confronted religious hypocrisy, was tried and crucified, and rose again. He fulfilled every prophecy, as the promised Messiah.

During His earthly life, He set an example for His followers of a simple, steady cadence of life. He completed His task on earth without worry or hurry. We can do the same.

Jesus—Our example

How did you spend your time last week? To answer, you might have to consult whatever tool you use to keep track of your schedule: a palm pilot, a pocket calendar, or the scribbled-on calendar on your refrigerator. Jesus Christ didn't have any of these, but as we read the Gospels, we can mark the passing of His days.

95

1. Jesus used His time well. Read Mark 1:9–28, 35; 2:1–12, 14–17 and jot down some of His activities.

Did He loaf or waste time? Do you note any sense of hurry?

> In the biography of our Lord, nothing is more noticeable than the quiet, even poise of His life. Never flustered whatever happened, never taken off His guard, however assailed by men or demons, in the midst of fickle people, hostile rulers, faithless disciples—always calm, always collected. Christ, the hard worker indeed, but doing no more or no less than God had appointed Him, and with no restlessness, no hurry, no worry. Was ever such a peaceful life lived under conditions so perturbing? (*Behind the Ranges*, Geraldine Taylor, quoting J. O. Fraser, 191)

The following passages reveal the calm demeanor of the Savior.

2. Jesus had time for children. Read Mark 10:13–16. What simple gift did these parents ask for their children?

How did the disciples respond and why do you think they acted this way?

What did Jesus do for the children?

What does this scene teach us about Jesus' spirit and demeanor in comparison to that of the disciples?

_____

_____

3. Jesus had time for individuals. Read John 4:3–10. What were Jesus' physical needs?

_____

_____

One lonely woman came to the well. What did Jesus do?

_____

_____

What kind of spirit did He show, even when tired and hungry?

_____

_____

4. Read Mark 5:22–34. Who came seeking Jesus' help for his desperately sick child?

_____

This man was a man of status, "one of the rulers of the synagogue." What was the scene like as Jesus went to his house?

_____

_____

For whom did He stop on the way and what did He do?

_____

What does this teach us about Jesus Christ?

_____

_____

5. Jesus had time for His friends. What friends are mentioned in Luke 10:38–42? What were they doing?

_____

_____

6. In John 21:1–14 what was Jesus doing and with whom?

_____

_____

7. Jesus took time for Himself. Read Matthew 14:23, Luke 6:12, and Mark 1:35. What was Jesus doing in these passages?

_____

_____

Children, needy people, friends, prayer—we know we too should make these a priority, but they are often neglected for lack of time. Discover Jesus' time-management secret, found in John 6:38—"For I came down from heaven, not to do mine own will, but the will of him that sent me."

That's the key to His steady, unhurried progress through His earthly years. Do you find yourself in a continual hurry, frazzled by a complicated, out-of-control schedule? Maybe you are doing some things that are only your will, not God's.

If a task or activity is in God's will for you, will He provide the time and energy to do it? Of course! If it's God's will for you to do it, you will always have time to do it, to do it well (and to sleep, too). At some seasons of life, of course, the world spins faster than usual (weddings, new babies, illness, Christmas). But if your daily agenda is continuously jam-packed, and you never come anywhere near the end of your to-do list, you may have added activities that are simply your will (or others' choices for you), not His.

You might be doing too much if

• you've never seen the bottom of your laundry hamper.

- clothes that have to be ironed are always worn warm.
- the pizza delivery guys know your dog's name.
- by the time you sew on the button, your child has outgrown the shirt.
- all your cookbooks feature "15-minute meals."

If you commit yourself to doing only God's will, what difference will it make when you're asked to add a new task to your list? What should you do before accepting any new responsibility or opportunity?

8. Write down a good (and godly) answer to give the next time you're asked, "Would you . . . ?"

_____

_____

Frenzy—A modern problem

Until railroads linked America's coasts and connected our cities, knowing the exact time didn't matter much. Daily life was controlled not by the exact hour but by the sun. The seasons, not the precise date, set the rhythm of work and leisure.

But with the trains came the need to know the correct time. Schedules had to be kept. About this same time, the telegraph made it possible to synchronize clocks across the country. And for many, time then became a tyrant.

Modern inventions make our lives more convenient and efficient. But sometimes devices that should be our slaves become our masters instead.

9. Can you think of ways that the following items can consume time, rather than saving it?

Cell phone

_____

Television

_____

Car

_____

Computer

_____

One day when I asked a child to check the mail, he responded with a question I didn't expect: "Which one?" Rather than just one "snail mail" arriving once a day, I realized we were now responsible for also checking and answering voice mail on two phones and e-mail on two computers. Our workload had been multiplied by our conveniences.

There was a time when having status meant having leisure. Today, however, many tie their significance to their busyness. Some even take pride in being too busy to cook, too busy to read, too busy to sleep. What are you too busy to do?

10. What good, profitable, God-pleasing activities have you recently neglected for lack of time?

_____

_____

11. Why do we believe that the busier we are, the more significant we are?

_____

_____

Maybe too much busyness does not please God. Maybe hurry is not part of God's will for His children.

Hurry—A thief

Just like any thief, hurry steals treasures. A complicated schedule that requires you always to be in a rush will steal from you.

12. Hurry steals quality of work. Read Colossians 3:22–24. To whom was Paul writing?

_____

These directions are given for household workers to follow in doing their daily routine. Who plays that role in your home?

13. How are we to do our "home" work?

_____

_____

Work in "singleness of heart." What does that mean?

_____

_____

You then can anticipate a reward from Whom?

_____

_____

Quality of work, even housework, matters to God. When you do "servant's work" diligently, as a service to the Lord, not for people, He is pleased with your faithfulness, and you will receive His reward.

When you're in a hurry, how do you do your work? When that happens, what has hurry stolen from you?

14. Hurry steals health. Read 1 Corinthians 6:19–20. You are told to give God glory in your _____ and in your spirit, for they both belong to _____.

15. What kind of physical body gives God (its Creator) glory?

_____

_____

Obviously, there are some things about your physical self that you can't control. But there is much that you can influence by your behavior.

16. How does being in a hurry affect

your diet?

_____

your exercise routine?

_____

your sleep?

_____

your grooming?

_____

Are you always running around "like a chicken with his head cut off"? Remember where he's headed—KFC!

Hurry steals the fruit of the Spirit. Read Galatians 5:22–26. The Holy Spirit wants to show Himself to others. These verses give nine evidences (fruits) of His presence, and they are all contrary to natural human behavior. When you display His fruit, you show that you are different—that you have the Holy Spirit living inside.

It's very easy to walk in the flesh rather than in the Spirit. The temptation to act like any other sinner will be especially strong when you are rushed.

17. When you are in a hurry, what does your behavior show?

Not love, but

_____

Not joy, but

_____

Not peace, but

_____

Not longsuffering, but

_____

Not gentleness, but

_____

Not goodness (good manners), but

_____

Not faith (faithfulness), but

_____

Not meekness, but

_____

Not temperance (self-control), but

_____

Hurry steals fellowship with God. Read Luke 10:38–42. Jesus was visiting in the home of His friends, the sisters Martha and Mary and their brother Lazarus. His disciples were probably with Him.

18. What was Martha doing?

_____

Was Martha doing wrong? No, it was both kind and necessary to provide a meal for her guests. But she may have been trying to entertain and impress rather than simply to be hospitable.

19. Find words in verses 40–41 that may indicate that she was doing more than was necessary.

_____

_____

20. While Martha scurried, what did Mary do?

_____

_____

Jesus praised Mary for making a good choice, for doing the one thing that was needful. Martha did what was good but temporary. Mary did what was essential and eternal.

If you get up late, what do you skip? Devotions, probably—promising yourself that you'll do it later. Just as it happened with Martha, the urgent takes priority over the necessary. If you are always in a hurry, you will never sit at His feet—and that, according to Jesus, is the only needful thing.

Where on today's to-do list is "sitting at Jesus' feet"? Has the thief of hurry stolen that privilege from you?

Change—A possibility

Here's how to escape the "busyness trap."

Commit yourself to honoring the Sabbath principle.

21. Humans were created on the sixth day of creation. What was established on the seventh day (Genesis 2:2–3)?

———————————————————————

Under the Old Testament law, there were strict rules for keeping the Sabbath. The Pharisees added hundreds more. Those laws aren't in effect today. In fact, Jesus rebuked those Jews who had perverted the Sabbath into a burden and not a blessing. But the Sabbath principle still exists.

Why did God originally set aside this special day? One purpose of the day was *worship.*

22. Who set the example for consistent public worship one day a week (Luke 4:16)?

———————————————————————

23. This same One declared Himself in Mark 2:27–28 to be ——————————————— of the Sabbath and explained that the Sabbath was made for the benefit of His creatures.

You weren't created to serve the Sabbath; it was created for your benefit. You were not created to run full-steam, full-time.

24. What fraction of your waking hours were your body and mind designed, at creation, to rest?

———————————————————————

Since the Resurrection, believers have honored the Lord's Day as a day of private rest and public church worship.

Sunday is not a day when you can't, but a day when you don't have to! You don't have to work but are free to rest. You are not bound by daily routine and concerns but can enjoy the calming release of fellowship with believers and worship of your Savior. You can rest your body from your normal workload. You can rest your spirit by focusing on the eternal rather than the temporal.

25. Recall last Sunday at your house.

    Was it restful?

    _____

    Was it worshipful?

    _____

26. What changes—in meals, in chores, in recreation, in use of media—can you make in your home to make Sunday more like the day of rest and worship it should be?

    _____

    _____

    _____

Schedule peaceful hours on the other days of the week too—hours that create a calm heart. Schedule times for private worship, thinking about God, and meditating on His Word. Honor the Sabbath principle every day.

Rest may be active—doing what you enjoy, doing whatever rests your mind and spirit—anything that's different from your usual work and relaxing to you. It may be reading, embroidery, baking, playing the piano or even pulling weeds! If you commit yourself to honoring the Sabbath principle, you'll find a way to do it. Try it and see how a rested heart transforms your face, your health, your marriage, your home, and your walk with God.

Lesson 11 A Weeping Heart

Pilgrimages to Jerusalem were a regular, joyful part of life in Bible times. Families traveled in a convoy of friends, chatting and singing psalms as they walked, eating and camping by the road. Sometimes the road was smooth and easy; other times it was rough and steep.

At some point along the road, although we don't know just where, the road passed through a gloomy valley. A shrub (maybe a mulberry or balsam), with seeping gum or with thorns, may have grown there. That place, known as the Valley of Baca, is used in Psalm 84 as a symbol for a desolate place, a place of suffering and pain: Baca, the valley of weeping.

On your pilgrimage, you too will pass through valleys of weeping. Your heart—your emotional self—will ache, and you will cry.

> *Therefore is my spirit overwhelmed within me; my heart within me is desolate.*
> *(Psalm 143:4)*

But be encouraged—in this dreary place, the pilgrims found a well of sweet, refreshing water. God's grace will be such a well for you during your trials. His loving presence will give you hope and comfort, keeping you from despair.

Blessed is the man whose strength is in thee; in whose heart are the ways of them. Who passing through the valley of Baca make it a well; the rain also filleth the pools. (Psalm 84:5–6)

THE TIMES FOR TEARS

Right times to cry

Read these Scriptures to find out when it's acceptable to cry.

1. Who was crying and why?

   John 11:32–36

   _____

   Acts 9:36–39

   _____

   Genesis 23:2

   _____

   John 20:11

   _____

   Matthew 2:16–18

   _____

   What's the *first* valid time for tears?

   _____

2. Who was crying and why?

   Psalm 42:3, 9–10

   _____

   1 Samuel 1:5–10

   _____

   What's the *second* valid time for tears?

   _____

3. Who wept and why?

Matthew 26:69–75

_____

Ezra 9:13–10:1

_____

Luke 7:36–38

_____

What's the *third* valid time for tears?

_____

4. According to Romans 12:15, when is another time to cry?

_____

What's the *fourth* valid time for tears?

_____

5. Who was weeping and why?

Luke 19:41–44

_____

Acts 20:29–31

_____

What's the *fifth* valid time for tears?

_____

6. What promise is given in Psalm 126:6?

_____

What's the *sixth* valid time for tears?

_____

Women also cry for other reasons. Some tears are sentimental and harmless (like tears during weddings and touching Hallmark commercials). Some are simply human, like tears during physical pain or at a great disappointment.

Wrong times to cry

Our tears can also have fleshly, sinful motivations. At times some women use tears as a weapon or tool of manipulation.

7. List other times when tears would not be pleasing to God.

_____

_____

God brought young Queen Esther to the court of King Ahasuerus at just the right moment to protect the Jews from murderous Haman. Their survival depended on the poise and courage of this queen. She cried at only one point during these stressful days—that we know of!

8. Those tears are recorded in Esther 8:3–6. Compare them to her spirit in Esther 4:16.

_____

_____

What can you learn from her example about the difference between legitimate tears and sinful ones?

THE USES OF TEARS

The Valley of Baca is any place of weeping—any place of trials. When you are going through a trial, you may ask, "Why is God letting this happen to me? He sees what is happening. He has power to change it. He says He loves me, so why does He let me suffer? Why does He let my heart cry?"

Those are reasonable questions. Some of the Lord's choicest servants have asked them—and they have found answers.

God allows your pain for His glory
Read 2 Corinthians 12:7–10.

9. What two symbolic names did Paul use to describe his trial?

_____

_____

To "buffet" literally means to hit with a fist. Paul felt beaten up! He begged the Lord three times to take away his suffering. But by the end of this passage, there's a startling change in his attitude.

10. What was his new outlook?

_____

Did Paul take pleasure in pain itself?

_____

If not, what did give him joy?

_____

Which did Paul value more: personal comfort or the glory of God?

Read 1 Peter 4:13–14. Peter tells his readers, who were suffering, that they were "partakers," or partners, in Christ's sufferings.

11. What did he mean by that?

_____

_____

When will those who suffer be "glad . . . with exceeding joy"?

_____

12. When will that be? Read Romans 8:17.

_____

Your spirit during sufferings can also bring Him honor on earth among those who do not believe on Him. When you handle trials in a God-glorifying way, He gets glory, as the world notices a different spirit in you, "the spirit of glory and of God."

Which do you value more: personal comfort or the glory of God?

Satan told God that Job served Him only because God had made him prosperous. He made this challenge.

> *But put forth thine hand now, and touch all that he hath, and he will curse thee to thy face. (Job 1:11)*

But instead,

> *Job blessed . . . the name of the Lord. In all this Job sinned not, nor charged God foolishly. (1:21–22)*

God then allowed Satan to "touch his bone and his flesh" (2:5). Job's faith survived even this excruciating pain. Seeing his suffering, his wife suggested that he commit suicide. She was talking, as Job said, "as one of the foolish women speaketh."

Job's faith grows throughout this fascinating book. Imagine the scene in heaven the next time Satan came to present himself before the Lord (1:6).

13. How did Job's testing bring God glory in heaven?

_____

_____

   On earth?

_____

_____

Which did Job value more: personal comfort or the glory of God?

14. Have you ever seen God's glory displayed in the midst of tragedy? Briefly describe a time.

_____

_____

_____

God allows your pain for your good

Sometimes trials are part of God's discipline—a way of rebuking you so that you will acknowledge and forsake sin. Search Hebrews 12:5–10 for answers to these questions.

15. What two things are you not supposed to do when the Lord chastens you through pain?

    _____

    _____

    What do those words mean in practical terms?

    _____

    _____

Here are two reasons to rejoice even in chastening.

16. God's discipline proves something about your relationship with Him. What is it (verses 6–9)?

    _____

    If you continuously sin without God's correction, what does that say about you?

    _____

    _____

17. His chastening has two worthwhile goals for your good. What are they (verses 10–11)?

    _____

    _____

Jonah did not want to do what God told him to do, so he ran away! God used two tools to chasten Jonah for his disobedience: a great tempest in the sea (Jonah 1:4) and a great fish to swallow him up (1:17). It took Jonah three long days and nights in that fish's smelly belly to learn his lesson.

18. What two good things did Jonah do when his "soul fainted" (2:7)?

_____

_____

He finally did what God asked him to do in the first place (Jonah 3). God's chastening produced good fruit in Jonah's life.

How do you know if your trial is God's chastening for sin or for some other purpose?

Pain makes you Christlike

Do you have a goal for your life? God does! It's found in Romans 8:29. To what are you "predestinated"?

> It behoved [was necessary for] Christ to suffer. (Luke 24:46)

> I lay down my life for the sheep. (John 10:15)

> Christ . . . hath given himself for us an offering and a sacrifice. (Ephesians 5:2)

> He humbled himself, and became obedient unto death. (Philippians 2:8)

> Learned he obedience by the things which he suffered. (Hebrews 5:8)

According to these Scriptures, what was Christ's earthly life like?

> He is despised and rejected of men; a man of sorrows, and acquainted with grief: and we hid as it were our faces from him; he was despised, and we esteemed him not. (Isaiah 53:3)

19. Christ suffered to atone for our sins. According to 1 Peter 2:21, what was another purpose of His suffering?

_____

_____

To become Christlike, you must go through suffering because that's what He did.

Pain develops your character

20. List some of the usual means of Christian growth.

_____

_____

Did you include trials in your list? Suffering teaches lessons that cannot be learned any other way. Your trials can be trails that lead to spiritual maturity.

21. Read 1 Peter 5:10, and then write it in your own words.

_____

_____

Patience grows during trials.

22. Fill in the missing words in the following verses.

Romans 5:3—"Tribulation worketh [produces]

_____."

James 1:3—"The trying of your faith worketh

_____."

James 5:10–11—"Ye have heard of the _____ of Job."

23. When Jesus suffered, what did He refuse to do, according to 1 Peter 2:21–23?

_____

_____

What did He do instead?

_____

Maturity develops during trials. According to James 1:2–4, trials → patience → maturity.

The trying [testing for trustworthiness] of your faith [your reliance on Christ's truth] worketh [accomplishes, works out] patience [cheerful endurance].

When you willingly allow the maturing process to go on, the result is that you become mature ("perfect") and complete, lacking nothing.

Which trial in your life "grew you up" the most quickly? Why was it so effective?

Faith is purified during trials. Through trials, your faith is tried by fire, like the precious metals silver and gold (Psalm 66:10 and 1 Peter 1:7). The wonderful final result of this testing is glory, honor, and praise to God.

24. What's the difference between professed faith and tested faith?

_____

_____

And I will bring the third part through the fire, and will refine them as silver is refined, and will try them as gold is tried: they shall call on my name, and I will hear them: I will say, It is my people: and they shall say, The Lord is my God. (Zechariah 13:9)

THE WAY TO HANDLE TEARS

Welcome them as friends

Because trials

- will purify you from sin.

- will make you more like Christ.

- will develop your character.

Then you can do what seems impossible—reckon them nothing but joy!

Count it all joy when ye fall into divers [different sorts of] temptations. (James 1:2)

A trial is not a muddy pit. It's a ladder to Christlikeness.

Look forward to the end of trials

One of the glories of heaven will be release from pain.

And God shall wipe away all tears from their eyes; and there shall be no more death, neither sorrow, nor crying, neither shall there be any more pain: for the former things are passed away. (Revelation 21:4)

When you're in severe trouble, when your heart groans and your eyes weep, look up to heaven. Praise Him for reminding you that because you know Him, someday all your crying will end. What glory that will be! Pain on earth makes His children long for their heavenly home.

Allow them to draw you nearer to your Lord

He has cautioned that in this world you'll have troubles, burdens, and anguish (John 16:33). He knows that there are some thorny Valleys of Baca that cannot be traversed without pain. Read these Scriptures out loud. They are as true for you as they were for the children of Israel.

When you cry, He sees your tears.

Thou tellest my wanderings: put thou my tears into thy bottle; are they not in thy book? (Psalm 56:8)

And the Lord said, I have surely seen the affliction of my people which are in Egypt, and have heard their cry by reason of their taskmasters; for I know their sorrows. (Exodus 3:7)

When you cry, He is with you.

In all their affliction he was afflicted, and the angel of his presence saved them: in his love and in his pity he redeemed them; and he bare them, and carried them all the days of old. (Isaiah 63:9)

Even if no one else knows or cares!

When my spirit was overwhelmed within me, then thou knewest my path . . . I looked on my right hand, and beheld, but there was no man that would know me: refuge failed me; no man cared for my soul. I cried unto thee, O Lord: I said, Thou art my refuge. (Psalm 142:3–5)

When you cry, He understands.

Lesson 12 A Submissive Heart

Submission. Is that your least favorite word? Does it call to mind a mousy woman cowering before a domineering husband? Does it arouse rebellious instincts as you envision a turned-off brain and trampled will? Did you almost decide to skip this lesson?

God's Word fearlessly uses this word, for godly submission to authority, from a yielded heart, pleases God. Be brave! As you study, you will discover that submission is much less negative and much more rewarding than you have thought.

THE MODERN VIEW OF SUBMISSION

1. Write your own definition of submission.

_____

_____

_____

Now, look it up in a dictionary. How was your definition different?

_____

_____

A submissive, compliant, humble, surrendered spirit is not generally regarded as a virtue by this generation. What qualities are desired and honored instead?

2. What is it about the "American dream" that makes a submissive heart seem undesirable?

_____

_____

_____

_____

Though this truth is currently unpopular, it is biblical. Let's see what God says about submission.

BIBLE SUBMISSION

Submission to _____ *(James 4:7; Romans 6:13)*

"And shalt return unto the Lord thy God, and shalt obey his voice according to all that I command thee this day, thou and thy children, with all thine heart, and with all thy soul." (Deuteronomy 30:2)

3. Who are two examples of this kind of submission?

Matthew 26:39

_____

Luke 1:38

_____

4. What words in the model prayer recorded in Matthew 6:10 say that you must pray with a submissive spirit?

_____

_____

_____

And whatsoever we ask, we receive of him, because we keep his command-ments, and do those things that are pleasing in his sight. (1 John 3:22)

Submission to _____ *(Colossians 3:20)*

5. Who is your example (Luke 2:48–52)?

_____

_____

At what point does this obligation cease?

_____

_____

Submission to _____ *(Romans 13:1–7)*

6. Who is your example (Mark 12:14–17; 15:15)?

_____

_____

Obedience to the government is obedience to God. The laws of the state (such as speed limits and tax laws) are God's laws and those who enforce them are God's ministers.

7. What does Romans 13:2 say about those who resist established laws?

_____

_____

What's the only exception to this rule (Acts 5:29)?

_____

_____

Submission to _____ *(Colossians 3:22)*

8. This passage was written to slaves who worked as household servants. Today's "masters" are employers. With what attitude, and what motivation, are you supposed to submit to them?

_____

_____

Submission to _____ *(Ephesians 5:21;*
   Philippians 2:3; 1 Peter 5:5)

9. What kind of heart attitude should you have when you're involved in group decision-making or in any sort of conflict?

_____

_____

First Peter 3:22 says this about Jesus Christ:

> *Who is gone into heaven, and is on the right hand of God; angels and authorities and powers being made subject unto him.*

10. Was Jesus submissive to His Father, to human government, and to His parents because He was inferior to them?

_____

If not, why was He submissive?

_____

_____

_____

Submission in _____ *(Genesis 2:21–24)*

Submission within marriage began at creation, when God created marriage. As its Creator, He gets to make the rules! His definition of marriage is the union of one man and one woman—a permanent, monogamous relationship.

> ### ONE MAN + ONE WOMAN = ONE FLESH

Within this oneness of marriage, there is an order of authority established by God for His glory and our blessing.

11. What was "not good," according to Genesis 2:18?

_____

_____

Adam lived in the perfect Garden of Eden. He knew and had named every other earthly creature, but still he was incomplete.

12. What did he lack (Genesis 2:20)?

_____

_____

13. How would a helper who was "meet" for (suited to, comparable to) him be different from animals?

_____

_____

God knew that Adam needed a feminine counterpart. Neither the garden nor Adam was complete without her! What uniquely feminine traits and strengths bring blessing to the world, the church, and the home?

14. Of what did God create the first woman (Genesis 2:21)?

_____

15. Compare this to Genesis 2:7. How was the first man created?

_____

_____

After creating Eve, God presented her to Adam as His gift (Genesis 2:22).

The sequence of God's creative acts points us to a woman's submissive role.

16. According to 1 Corinthians 11:8–9, who was made for whom?

_____

_____

17. Adam named his mate. What did he call her and why (Genesis 2:23)?

_____

_____

The man (*ish*) called her woman (*ishshah*). Later he named her "Eve" (Genesis 3:20). Adam took pleasure in Eve. Made from his side, created as his perfect companion, she was his delight. This was the ideal marriage: a husband who loved and cared for his wife and a wife who was his willing helper and friend.

Distorted by sin

Satan, the deceitful serpent, came to Eve as a creature of dazzling beauty. Alone, without the protection and counsel of her husband, she gave in to the serpent's urging to disobey God and eat of the forbidden fruit. She was deceived. But Adam, knowing exactly what he was doing, violated God's command.

18. Underline the words in these verses that reveal the difference between Eve's choice and Adam's.

    For Adam was first formed, then Eve. And Adam was not deceived, but the woman being deceived was in the transgression. (1 Timothy 2:13–14)

At that moment, sin entered paradise. Everything changed, including marriage. Following God's plan of godly leadership and joyful submission is now so difficult that marriage often degenerates into a battleground of two selfish wills. Every married couple needs God's help and power to have a happy, biblical marriage.

God described the new situation in Genesis 3:16: "Unto the woman he said . . . thy desire shall be to thy husband, and he shall rule over thee."

The word *desire* indicates that a wife would now want to rule over her husband. Since the day sin entered the world, wives have subtly undermined their husbands' authority or openly demanded to command the home.

God's design for husbands has been perverted as well. Instead of leading with love, kindness, and wisdom, recognizing a wife's unique value and full equality in Christ, sinful men have often become domineering and abusive, considering their wives inferior, ruling as tyrants.

The consequences of the fall have been tragic. God's plan for marriage is for your good, with two partners fulfilling their roles in a union of loving hearts. Only with God's help can your marriage resemble His original design!

Described in the New Testament

19. First Corinthians 11:3 summarizes God's chain of authority. What is it?

_____

_____

_____

How can you tell that this list doesn't depict superiority and inferiority?

_____

_____

20. Read Ephesians 5:22–24. What qualifications are placed on this command?

_____

_____

Do differences in education, intellect, character, or spirituality alter this mandate?

_____

_____

When a wife submits to her husband, she is ultimately submissive to the Lord.

21. What comparisons are made in verse 23? The husband is the _____ of the wife, just as _____ is the _____ of the church. The husband is the _____ of the wife's body, just as Christ is the Savior of the church.

What does a "savior" do? How can a godly husband "save" his wife? Some of his obligations are listed in Ephesians 5:25–33. A husband provides security by protecting his wife from pain and shielding her from want. He meets her physical needs and comforts her in trials.

22. Therefore (because a husband is like Christ and a wife like His church), what should a wife do (verse 24)?

_____

_____

What's the only exception (Acts 5:29)?

_____

_____

Wives, submit yourselves unto your own husbands, as it is fit in the Lord.
(Colossians 3:18)

Submit is a military term expressing a soldier's deference to and respect for an officer, simply because of the rank he holds. What would these organizations be like without a structure of leadership? The military? A business? A city? A church?

23. What is a home like when husband and wife struggle for dominance and control?

_____

_____

_____

_____

Paul wrote his epistles in the days of the Roman Empire, when heathen husbands were often harsh tyrants over the wives they considered their slaves. Some women, in response, adopted a radical feminism that became widespread throughout the empire. There was therefore a need for believing wives to learn God's plan for the home.

24. Who was to teach the young women, according to Titus 2:3–5?

_____

_____

What were they to teach?

_____

If Christian wives follow God's pattern in the home, what will be the result?

_____

_____

Paul's writings on marriage did not degrade or devalue women. Instead, they elevated women into the beloved and protected wives of godly men who loved their wives as Christ loved the church.

In every organization, including the home, there is a need for input and discussion when decisions are being made. But the one "at the top" must be allowed to make the final decisions, for they will be held accountable.

> *Obey them that have the rule over you, and submit yourselves: for they watch for your souls, as they that must give account, that they may do it with joy, and not with grief: for that is unprofitable for you. (Hebrews 13:17)*

25. What great responsibility do your authorities have?

_____

_____

How can your willing submission help them?

_____

_____

Maybe you find it hard to obey authorities. You're not alone. Joyful surrender is never easy, for each of us has a heart that wants its own way and is sure its way is best. But sweetly submitting—especially when you'd rather not—will bring you great blessings, for it is God's will. And submitting will make you Christlike, which is the greatest reward of all.

MY TESTIMONY